futurehitdna.com

Funded by
MISSION COLLEGE
Carl D. Perkins Vocational and Technical Education Act Grant

FUTUREHIT.DNA

How the digital revolution is changing Top 10 songs

Jay Frank

Futurehit, Inc.

Published by Futurehit, Inc., Nashville, Tennessee

Library of Congress Cataloging-in-Publication Data

Frank,Jay
    Futurehit.dna: How the digital revolution is changing Top 10 songs / Jay Frank
        p.   cm.
    ISBN-13: 978-0-6152-8570-2
    ISBN-10:   0-6152-8570-8
    1.   Music business. 2. Music technology.

Manufactured in the United States of America by Lightning Source

For Alexandria Eve

TABLE OF CONTENTS

PROLOGUE

HOW THE FUTUREHIT

IDEA TOOK SHAPE

Technology dictates music creativity, not the other way around. These are words that every freethinking musician would likely vehemently deny. If you are a musician reading this right now, you are probably thinking of a thousand contradictory statements:

- Music comes from the soul.
- The type of music that can be created is limitless.
- I am independent, so I can make whatever I want.
- When I create, I use technology. It does not lead me. I lead it.

I will not say that any of these statements are not true. They are. That is fine if music is nothing more than a hobby. Yet for many of us, music is not a sideline gig. It is a profession. It can be a lucrative profession for some, a never-ending struggle as a starving artist for others. For many, it is somewhere in the middle. If you are going to think of music professionally and plan to make any money that might go toward paying the rent, you have to recognize that technology will dictate the type of music you create.

Radiohead's "Paranoid Android" is a fantastic, magical, complex song that I dearly love. But unless you are extraordinarily talented, can you sing that song around a campfire? Before the printing press, you mostly had to teach music in order for it to survive. Can you teach a group to memorize the full lyrics and melody of this song in a matter of minutes? Then there is the instrumentation, which could doubtfully be handled by a single human being in a song leader scenario.

Oh, yeah. The instruments themselves are also technology. In the past century, we have taken for granted the guitar, piano, drums and woodwinds set as something that has been around forever. It has not. Every time a new instrument is added, modified and perfected into the technological stream, music changes forever. The lone exception is probably drums. But any drummer worth his salt will tell you that drums need to be tuned. I highly doubt the early bang-on-something drums the cavemen practiced on had any sense of predetermined tonality.

So when it comes to the ideas in this book, it is amazing to me that the angle in which these theories are addressed has, to my knowledge, never been examined. In my head, it is as if a trick mirror were suddenly discovered and re-angled so the light shone in a different way. The ideas behind *Futurehit.DNA* are certainly based on music as heard through the Internet, iPods, phones, and more. This is where we are today, and this is what will shape the immediate tomorrow. What turned out to amaze me is how the ideas also shone a light on the past, and how similar technological trends in the recorded music era (approximately the last 100 years) also made certain hit songs the standards we know today.

WHAT YOU REALLY WANT TO HEAR

As I think about my career and the experiences in it that shaped the direction of this book, I realize that I belong to a small group of music business gatekeepers who move the needle based on actual music listener activity. This may seem rather silly to an industry outsider, but most people would rather respond to insider information and "gut instinct" than what a consumer actually did. Occasionally, this produced legitimate hits, but most of the time produced the music that clogs up the dollar bins at used CD stores. Radio programmers try to gauge consumer interest through what is known as callout research. We will address why this, too, is a fallacy and does not accurately show consumer demand.

In all the leadership positions I held, I somehow got attracted to those that actually monitor consumer behavior and made decisions accordingly. The independent record label I worked at sprung out of a direct marketing company that utilized fan information to gauge success and direction. It also utilized the Internet to collect and gain immediate feedback from fans. and measured that volume to gauge success. In 1994, these procedures were embryonic, but radical in their approach.

From there, I went to the Box Music Network. This network, which ran from the mid-1980s until 2000, was a television video network whereby users could call a 900 number and a video would play. The slogan was, "Music Television You Control," and they did. The genius was that it was a national brand with a local feed. This meant that when you made your video request, it felt like it played for the whole country, but only played for your individual city.

Needless to say, this technology garnered extensive information. We could monitor when specific videos and songs were hot city by city. We could see what type of music was popular in individual cities. With advances in digital technology, we could fine-tune the programming so that the music was tailor made for that city. Local artists could be added only to one specific city and be as big of a hit as the chart toppers, although they played nowhere else in the country. By making programming decisions based on user data--coupled with the precise geographical pinpointing we could do through digital technology--we doubled the audience viewership in eighteen months, sold records, and made many new stars.

That experience led me to LAUNCH, which soon became Yahoo! Music. The crew was weathering the dot-com bust, because they wanted to give the right music to the right people. They had developed the innovative radio service called LAUNCHcast, which aggregated community response to songs, and subsequently pushed them to people predisposed to like them. This produced a radio station that was custom tailored to your exact musical tastes. It quickly became the most listened to online radio service in the world. Applying the same approach to music videos also spawned the largest online music video service, before the introduction of YouTube.

All this activity led to a multitude of data points that, when looked at as a whole, could often predict what songs were most likely to become hits. This meant that Yahoo! Music played songs as hits well before they were recognized as such. It also provided an opportunity to punch holes in anointed "gatekeeper" songs, and predict with stunning accuracy when a song would *not* become a hit, and/or when a song would not sell records. The accuracy came from many points, which included both their explicit actions around an artist or song, as well as their implicit actions. We could not only determine which songs people liked, but also how they liked them, and if that would lead to a consumer purchase.

After awhile, when you looked at data consistently, you started to see patterns. In a brief period of time, these patterns started jumping out The speed at which most people gave new music a chance. The fact that people had very little room for mediocre songs. Certain styles and songs would inspire people to make a purchase while others, equally as popular, would leave people satisfied in just hearing them and not owning them.

It did not take a long time to see certain elements within songs that consistently showed up. These elements were also consistent among genres, age groups, and usage patterns. I found that applying them to easily recognized patterns of public behavior, both in and around music, only reinforced the similarities that were springing up.

As I started to put these ideas into practice, and speak about them to music business insiders, the results varied widely. Some people immediately grasped the concepts, while others dismissed them completely. Yet as time grew, the concepts only got reinforced. More and more songs that went on to become successful hits, both chart wise and financially, fit the model.

THE TRUE TECHNOLOGY CHANGES IN MUSIC

To me, it has been incredible to watch consultants and experts talk about the changes the various technologies have brought. Virtually none of these experts, though, talked about the changes to the music itself. When it was about the music, the focus was on such topics as the Beatles' leaving money off the table by not licensing their music or some variation thereof. I think some lived in an idealized world, i.e the new landscape would allow previously underground stars to become mainstream. (See Stereogum and other sites of its ilk.) Others ignored the changes, as there was still plenty of money to be made by the old radio-and-retail push if it were done right.

This left the gaping hole of what was truly happening. The listening patterns, combined with overall inundation from many other forms of entertainment, have changed the game. It is no longer about tweaking the form to impress the gatekeeper. It is now about the quality of the music, coupled with subtle manipulations, to make sure the consumer has a chance to respond to the quality.

Needless to stay, the styles and structures of music have changed and will change in the near future. Nearly every technological breakthrough has led to new songwriting structures, new production techniques, and sometimes even new musical genres. It often takes five to ten years before these changes truly take place, but they do. If musicians, songwriters, and the industry do not embrace these changes in the next few years, they are almost certainly going to continue to experience financial hardships.

New usage patterns show that fifteen elements have emerged to influence which songs become popular and successful. It is unlikely that any one song will contain or utilize all fifteen elements. But it *is* likely that other elements will evolve over the next few years. And to achieve maximum success, a song will need several of the fifteen elements spelled out here.

This book is not meant as a guidebook to music as art. Musicians who wish to explore their music as art rightfully should ignore most, if not all of the precepts in this book. If a musician creates art, then he should be only slightly concerned about the business aspects. In most cases, his music almost by definition is not commercial, and therefore he should be unconcerned, if not downright rebellious, at the notions spelled out here.

This book is also not a substitute for talent. If someone does not have the abilities to craft basic theoretical music elements, adopting these precepts is not going to substantially make up for the lack of those core elements. Having those unique qualities is crucial in the making of a hit or popular song.

Musicians are generally looking for a balance between art and commerce, and for that, this book becomes an important guide. This is a new environment where anything goes. I am sure some artists and songs will succeed without embracing these ideas. The new rules certainly allow for that. In my experience, the failure to adopt at least some of these ideas will just make for a much steeper climb up the hill to a commercially rewarding hit. Other artists and songs will embrace these ideas wholeheartedly and still not achieve success. Implementing these points will do you no good unless the underlying talent and quality is already there.

Whether you are an artist, songwriter, producer, programmer, executive, or belong to any other profession that touches a song from inception to delivery, I truly hope that this book helps you make the subtle tweaks necessary to give you an advantage. For in this day and age, with the sheer volume of music that is accessible, you need every competitive edge you can get.

JAY
FRANK

NASHVILLE, TN

LOOKING BACK

FOR THE

NEW VIEW:

A QUICK HISTORY OF

MUSIC & TECHNOLOGY

Before technology, songs were sung live. People would gather, and usually a song leader would guide the assemblage in an easily understood tune: Simple words, chants, and easy rhyme schemes. You needed that because there was no printing press to produce song sheets, so the group had to learn the song quickly and easily. "Kumbaya" is the perfect example. You can probably remember most stanzas of "Kumbaya," just by mentioning the title. Over time, songs became more complex, like "Home on the Range." In these songs, the chorus is easily memorable, but the verses are not. This is where the song leader came in.

Over time, instruments were created to accompany these songs. Interestingly, certain notes virtually did not exist before the invention of specific instruments. But even when those notes came into existence, music stayed mostly within a comfortable three-octave range. Songs with ultra-high or low octaves were used to expand the dimension of music, and could not have even been thought up before technology created the instrument.

To reach a larger audience with these new octaves (or not), music needed to be amplified. Theatres were then created with sound projection in mind. This started with Greek theatres, and moved over time to more dynamic venues such as opera houses. Yet still, proper amplification with its resulting changes to music is only a recent phenomenon. To underscore the importance of this, think of the infamous Beatles concert in Shea Stadium in 1965. A rock show had never been attempted in a stadium before, and the band had to use the house PA system just to be heard. From most accounts, the band could not hear themselves, and the attendees could not hear much better. The acoustics of a baseball park are better suited to large crowd noises than to musicians with a public address system.

Fewer than ten years after that event, heavy metal music became popular, along with its attendant stacks of huge amplifiers. As the biggest band in the world, the Beatles would have had access to the best sound systems, yet a decade later many smaller bands had systems with much more power. What changed was the technology. Not only were the amplifiers themselves more powerful, but the ability to deliver more power to drive multiple amps was surely also developed. In the 1970s, it was still important to turn off all electronic devices after use, lest they accidentally start a house fire. Now, most people leave on multiple electronic devices all the time without considering such danger. That change in electricity distribution not only made homes safer, but it allowed loud musical genres such as heavy metal to be created.

The style of music was not the only thing that changed. So did the number of people who could hear that music live simultaneously. Venues were created that allowed tens of thousands of people to hear music. If you talked to many original Woodstock attendees about what music they heard, very few likely heard the music cleanly, if at all. The ability to stage Woodstock was a technological achievement in itself. A music gathering of more than the few thousand people a theatre could hold was not possible until recently. It is astounding to think of big jazz artists in the 1950s playing small clubs, or giants in the 1960s like Elvis Presley or Frank Sinatra playing Vegas theatres that were so small as to be considered side rooms in the modern casino. Yet in the 1970s, avant garde progressive rock acts like Emerson, Lake and Palmer or King Crimson could play in large arenas.

MASS DISTRIBUTION

While live performance has been around since music was created, mass distribution of music without the artist being present is actually a relatively new phenomenon. Edison invented the Gramophone a mere 130 years ago. At the time, you had to play or sing into a large horn 'o plenty and then pray the wax cylinders caught your music effectively. If you messed up...well, the cylinders were expensive, so you probably lived with it. For half a century, "mixing" in recorded music consisted of positioning the musician near the microphone for a one-take recording.

The same goes for piano, or Pianola rolls, which were popular entertainment in the late nineteenth century and early twentieth century. All a person had to do was thread the roll in the player, and a song played. In many ways, the piano roll was a performance. Someone would play a piece on a piano, a machine would punch holes for each note as it was being performed, and the punched holes would form the basis for mass-produced rolls.

As with the Gramophone, if you made a mistake, you often went with it. There was no splicing or editing. Piano rolls also could not be too thick, or they would not fit the machine. The piano roll length, therefore, determined the maximum length of a song through this medium. Since piano rolls were very well liked, the songs that could have been popular live, but extended for five minutes and beyond, were now out of the question for mass distribution. Three-minute songs became the accepted length, and music creators naturally gravitated to this technology's new limitation.

Piano rolls, however, were feared and derided by the music industry as a technology that was going to put people out of jobs. Piano players would no longer be able to find work. Sheet music would become extinct, as people no longer needed it. What occurred was actually the contrary. Publishers ended up making more money, as the formats complemented, instead of cannibalized, each other.

Around the same time, full-length classical pieces of a variety of lengths began to wane in popularity, since distribution was anything but guaranteed. Piano rolls and early records started to deliver early versions of "pop" songs. Folk songs, which were popular in rural areas and also considered "hillbilly" music, became big with upper-income demographics. The reason was easy: Folk was one of the only existing genres that could fit the length of piano rolls.

As piano rolls became an effective method to distribute popular music, many songs adapted what is now a standard "verse-chorus-verse-chorus" pattern. The main purpose for this was to make it easier for musicians and producers to mechanically reproduce the songs. If they could visually see where patterns in the song began and ended, manufacturing the piano rolls became much easier. Additionally, the idea for repeating the end of the chorus developed when musicians found themselves with paper left in a roll, and needed to fill the time. Most often, musicians would just repeat the chorus exactly, change the key, or raise the chorus up by one octave. What is now considered a standard convention derived from this need to fill up paper space.

At about the same time, the affordability of pianos in homes gave rise to the need for sheet music, and technology accelerated to allow its greater mass production. Also, with the industrial revolution in full swing, more people had new disposable income and leisure time that needed to be filled. The music publishing business quickly became an industry in which many people profited.

To grow this industry, songs had to be tailored to please the audience. They also had to be easy enough for amateurs to learn and perform. Long songs and symphonies were out. Folk songs, which had plenty of repetition, suited the mass market. Songs with vocals, simple arrangements, and lyrics that groups could easily learn, became more popular. The songs usually ended up being short, and the melody lines were not complicated, so anyone could join in without too much difficulty. Songs that did not embrace these rules were usually unpopular, and as a result did not earn money for the songwriters or publishers.

The songs that became popular were also reflected in the new diversity spreading through the United States. The late nineteenth century saw massive immigration from Europe. This led to quick dissemination of their indigenous music, such as Irish folk songs. Former slaves, who had been freed less than a generation earlier, were singing traditional spirituals in national tours of the U.S. Since these songs were mostly in the public domain, sheet music sold of these songs enjoyed higher profit margins. These are but a few examples of the results the changing demographic had when it intersected with the newly created music business.

As these formats thrived in popularity, the new phonograph technology was getting ready for mass production. This technological breakthrough did not come easily. Much like the VHS and Beta wars, early records were either on a phonograph cylinder (which had the "early to market" advantage), or a lateral-cut "Gramophone" disc. While the two formats fought, it became clear that cylinders were more expensive to reproduce. Once the patent for lateral-cut discs ran out at the end of 1918, its place as the format of choice was evident. Never mind that Gramophone players became commonly known as a "phonograph," much like any portable digital device or MP3 player is now called an iPod, irregardless of its manufacturer.

A third cylinder-type player called a "graphophone" also existed. It had a tough time competing until the Columbia Graphophone Company began leasing devices to fairgrounds, where patrons could play popular songs for a nickel. They were well-received and generated large profits. While technical limitations of the cylinders still kept the song length to less than three minutes, there was also no incentive to lengthen the songs. If songs were longer, fewer nickels would be collected throughout the day.

The lateral-cut discs took off when players were motorized, giving each record a standard speed. (The previous "hand crank" method produced uneven sound results.) The initial standard played a recorded work on a flat disc at 78 revolutions per minute (rpm). These records could be produced in a variety of diameters, ranging from seven inches all the way up to twenty-one inches. Because the common length of most songs from other mediums was two to three minutes, the ten-inch format became the standard, as it had a maximum length of three minutes. This allowed manufacturers to keep costs down, and created a subtle reinforcement of the three-minute song as standard.

These elements of music distribution collided to drive the creativity of musicians and songwriters. While there were more expensive ways to distribute titles longer than three minutes, they were not considered mass appeal. For the most part, this was confined to classical and opera. Perhaps early recording artists could have made more songs that supported much longer song lengths, but they wisely bowed to the conventional wisdom of a three-minute song. Today, musicians who wish to make a career out of their art may not have to conform to societal norms, but they do have to conform to technical limitations at the time of creation. Without that, the chances of any financial benefit from their career choice would be extremely low.

The Depression years brought huge change to music with the popularity of newer affordable forms of entertainment: Radio and films. In the early part of the century, the three-minute 78 rpm side was the only way to hear recorded music. When the radio gained prominence during the Depression, the consumer got all the music he wanted, along with news and other entertainment (such as radio dramas), at a one-time cost. With this, live music now enjoyed mass distribution, which allowed expansion of the three-minute song standard.

The rise of radio caused the recorded music industry to plummet. The Depression nearly put the final nail in the coffin, as records and their players were deemed non-essential items. With record sales nearly driven to extinction in those years longer songs began to find more opportunities.

Due to limited broadcasting and recording technologies, radio stations could not do things that are taken for granted today. An announcer saying the name of a song over the instrumental introduction could not happen easily. Ending the tune with a song fade was downright difficult at best. As a result, a lot of songs in this era start with the song's hook at the very first beat, or after an extremely short introduction. The songs also end with a big finish or definitive cold ending. This did not happen because of a stylistic choice of the early Tin Pan Alley writers or performers. It happened because that was the most effective way to do it.

While the early days of radio seemed poised to unshackle the length of an average song, advertisements became a necessity that hampered creative opportunities. Since the advertiser had to be mentioned in the broadcast at specific times, certain songs could not air, as their excessive length would bleed into the time owned by the advertiser. This, coupled with the length of the 78 rpm record, kept most songs short. The new market of songs written to help sell advertising in a short, quick burst added an additional reinforcement to the notion of a hit song being brief and catchy.

Film was not much better in offering limited musical choices, as film sound had not been around for ten years during the Depression years. Even the notion of sound editing was still a pipe dream. At that point, editing consisted of breaks where the dialogue ended and the song began. That is why most films with musical numbers in the 1930s begin the song precisely with a visual edit.

Even with these new technologies providing mass distribution of longer songs, the songwriters (not often the performers--publishers ruled in these days) did not get paid well from these outlets. They got paid from sheet music and record sales. While they suffered like everyone else at the time, there was still enough income for big writers. With no new technological breakthroughs in record pressing or printing, three minutes remained the acceptable length of a pop song, and most radio and movies followed suit.

In the ensuing years through the end of World War II, the business stayed alive through various marketing and cost-cutting attempts. A major advantage records had over free radio was sound quality, and this drove sales. Engineers and marketers worked feverishly to create new technologies and names that had sizzle in order to convince people to purchase records. The big development came when RCA switched from making records on shellac to PVC, or vinyl. This grew out of the shellac shortage during World War II, and allowed for fewer broken records, which meant less returned product and more profits.

After costs were managed, profit growth resulted from the mass rollout of the jukebox. While jukeboxes were always popular, there was no way to distribute them on a mass scale. It was the Wurlitzer Company that finally developed the best way to achieve that. By the end of the 1930s, with other companies jumping in, jukebox distribution increased twelve fold, and kept the record business afloat. The standard in these machines was the ten-inch record, which once again reinforced boundaries by which an artist could record a song. This circle of economic necessity drove artistic boundaries by what was realistic to profit from recorded music.

After World War II ended in the 1940s, and people found an economy ready to grow again, the climate was right for new technologies to be developed and bring changes to music creation. At this time, jazz, big band, blues, classical, and country/folk had remained relatively unchanged for some twenty years. Pop music took elements from any of those genres, depending on the song. The reality is that since technology made few advances, and economics kept these technologies from being modified or invented during the Depression and World War II, music remained largely unchanged during this time.

POST-WAR CHANGES

The new economic prosperity of the late 1940s and 1950s allowed for a flurry of technologies to be invented in a short period of time. These new elements were certainly catalysts in changing music creation. The most interesting battle took place in the 1950s, as manufacturers battled to come up with a new "standard" format for records. The battle wasn't just between 33 1/3 rpm twelve-inch records (LPs), or 45 rpm seven-inch records (45s). The battle was also figuring out ways to make the vinyl much cheaper, as well as decreasing the costs of the players themselves. Columbia and RCA, respectively, were successful on both fronts.

While LPs were a quick success in the classical, jazz and show tunes market, it was the 45 that dominated the pop market and defined the pop song structure. The affordability of the format--and ease of integration into the business-- made the 45 the new standard for the jukebox. As jukebox airplay was the predominant element driving the popular music charts in *Billboard*, any technological development in this area was going to dominate the industry. When jukeboxes converted from 78s to 45s, their increasing popularity, coupled with the technological limitations, continued to cement the idea of the three-minute song for consumers and artists alike. Jukeboxes were such a standard that the large center hole on 45s existed specifically to accommodate the technical need of efficient record switching. Thus, business concern trumped consumer convenience, and record buyers had to use inconvenient adapters to hear the music they purchased.

In the 1950s, a world of radical change occurred in recorded music, largely through a variety of advances in electronics. These technologies created a whole new genre of music (rock and roll), blurred versions of existing genres (most notably country and blues), and the mechanics in which these sounds were distributed.

The electric guitar (and the amplification of it) is what most would arguably call the single biggest element in this particular wave of change. The first electric guitars appeared in the mid-1930s, but with the Depression and World War II, mass distribution for the new technology was still far away. It took two companies, Gibson and Fender, to begin figuring out successful production techniques in the late 1940s and early 1950s. Throughout that process, the early models were imperfect. But by the time the Fender "Stratocaster" emerged in 1954, these problems were resolved, and the instrument became poised to take over the new developing sounds of country and rock.

The emergence of the electric guitar on its own did not change the way songs are written and structured. "Hound Dog" and countless other early rock hits were blues songs that had been around for several years. Even with rock's success at that time, artists like Pat Boone were producing far bigger and more consistent hits. Older wartime artists such as Frank Sinatra were experiencing not only career resurgences, but also climbing to all-time career highs.

In that regard, the single biggest electronic device that changed the way people listen to music was the much more modest sound mixer. This benign behind-the-scenes product was quickly integrated into many elements used in the music system.

Prior to this point, most radio DJs relied on one turntable and bantered as they changed records. Since DJs had to simultaneously act as announcers and engineers, it was nearly impossible for them to make seamless transitions between records. In party situations, DJs often employed a live drummer to keep the beat between songs.

Radio was transformed when it invested in updated mixers and multiple turntables in the studio. While Sir James Savile, working in England in the mid-1940s, made the first use of two turntables at once, it took nearly another decade for the concept to reach the U.S. Now, for the first time, energy levels could be manipulated, creating additional frenzied excitement for the music itself. Anticipation for music took on a new form based on the intros of the songs (or lack of them).

The DJ himself could even build this anticipation. With a lone turntable, the announcer had to bridge gaps of silence, so banter often consisted of elongated commercials or just gibberish. Attempting to talk coherently while efficiently changing a record is akin to rubbing your stomach and patting your head simultaneously. With two turntables, record changing was now done swiftly and easily. A song could be announced as it began to play, which increased the excitement and merchandised the song more efficiently for eventual purchase.

With one turntable, DJs had a huge task in keeping up energy levels between songs, and often leaned on records that enabled them to spike that energy. That, in turn, required artists to make records that played into this needed element. One notable technique was a "clarion call" to start a song. "Rock Around the Clock," with its "1-2-3-o'clock, 4-o'clock rock" open, helped define the style. But it was far from the only major hit to do this. Elvis Presley practically built his career with bold opening *a cappella* statements: "You ain't nothin' but a hound dog" ("Hound Dog"), and, "Well, since my baby left me" ("Heartbreak Hotel"), and "Well, a hard-headed woman, a soft-hearted man" ("Hard Headed Woman"). These declarations capitalized on the energy the DJ brought, and demanded that the listener pay attention. It's no wonder each of those songs went to #1 in the U.S.

The length of the song was also crucial. DJs liked songs that were 2 1/2 minutes long, mostly because they allowed them to continue that energy and momentum. Not surprisingly, the average length of a #1 song in the first three years of the rock era (1955-1957) was two minutes and twenty-nine seconds. As noted before, there really was not much a DJ could do about the length of a song, because songs could not physically be more than three minutes long on one side of a record. But even here technology paved the way. The development of vinyl records led not just to the 45, but also the LP.

The commerce advantages of the 45 record were extremely noteworthy. The more durable vinyl was smaller, a plus in shipping and displays. It also made mass sales and distribution easier, and brought down costs--affording the new baby boomers entering their teen years a cheap way to get music. However, the cost cutting came at a price, as sound quality on these discs was poorer than 78s or LPs, due to the compression on the groove. Yet, as today's MP3 tracks prove, youth's consumption of music is about convenience and affordability, and not quality.

The listening habits changed when the durability of vinyl resulted in the record changer. The user could now place several records on a stack and play them all in a row without getting up to change them. These devices first appeared for 78 rpm records in the late twenties, but due to the Depression, they never became a mass consumer item. The

1950s and the new popular record formats quickly made this a standard feature on many turntables.

At first glance, the record changer seems nothing more than a footnote. In fact, it is quite the contrary. Playlisting on an iPod might not have existed without the record changer. Up until this widespread adoption in the 1950s, passive music entertainment was solely found on the radio. Like today, this was a decent, but largely unsatisfactory way to experience music, due to constant announcer interruptions, advertisements, and the inability to select what music was to be played next. Because record sides were limited to either three-minute segments or live performances, the notion of music as "background" did not exist.

Think about this for a minute. Fifty years later, we accept that music is a background of nearly every portion of our lives. Shopping. Commuting. House cleaning. Eating dinner. Having sex. Yet in the broader history of music, the act of listening to music in the background is something entirely new to the way one is supposed to hear it. But with the advent of the record changer, everything began to change. The listener could control the order in which he wanted to hear songs. He could listen to about thirty minutes of 45s with minimal interruption between songs. Best of all, the listener could completely control his environment of music *and* perform other tasks while listening. With this addition (coupled with car radio's arrival), the notion of music as a background element began to grow exponentially to the main form of music listening today.

The LP record also grew in the 1950s as a popular format that changed listening habits, as it moved from the world of classical, jazz, and show tunes into the realm of pop and rock. At lengths of approximately fifteen minutes per side, initial pop LP releases were merely collections of previously recorded singles. As such, most songs on albums were two-to-three minutes long. At fifteen minutes a side, it was presumed that albums were ten songs. While many LPs expanded this notion (with some classical and show tune records coming close to thirty minutes per side), it did not generally move beyond this structure for pop music until the mid-1960s, more than fifteen years after the LP came to the mass market.

THE FAB FOUR

Consider the Beatles. They have long been considered the leaders in changing music during the mid-1960s. Their initial albums were all released in this general format: Fourteen songs that ran a total of thirty-three to thirty-four minutes, with each song averaging two minutes and twenty seconds, to two minutes and thirty seconds per album. While almost all of their songs were explicitly recorded for an album, and not a single release, the songs were so interchangeable that the first three years of the Beatles' recording career brought entirely different albums in the U.K. than in the U.S. Each U.S. release was eleven or twelve songs, and averaged less than thirty minutes. Additionally, singles were released with regularity. Different song orders, different album titles--this was the norm for the first half of the Beatles' career.

Even though the band hated the U.S. reordering of their material, the reality was they were making solid, interchangeable singles averaging the standard length of just under 2 1/2 minutes. And who had the time to do anything different? The Beatles were on a whirlwind trip--performing for screaming girls and a worldwide fan base that grew so quickly it has never been duplicated.

In 1967, this led to the album that established a new outlook for the LP release: *Sgt. Pepper's Lonely Hearts Club Band*. The album was not just a collection of challenging pop arrangements, with classical instruments, choirs, genre shifts, and quirky rhythms. It also broke the mold for song lengths, offering up a huge variety of running times. Songs blended together right from the start, which was complete heresy to pop song delivery. The end of the album had a one chord piano fade out that, at seventy-three seconds, is half the length of the average Beatles hit.

Sgt. Pepper's... shattered accepted structure standards and allowed bands and artists to reinvent themselves. It is considered a high point of 1960s art, because it proved that pop artists could embrace artistic challenges outside of the boundaries that made them popular. From that point forward, the album format offered new, untapped potential for pop music beyond a collection of standard two minute and thirty second pop singles.

When *Sgt. Pepper's...* successfully changed the notion of song lengths on albums, the Beatles directly challenged the length of the single the very next year. In 1968, the Beatles asked radio to play all seven minutes and four seconds of "Hey Jude." This move took a sledgehammer to the three-minute standard. Up until that point, only five pop songs that were over four minutes long had reached #1, and none had succeeded over five minutes. This groundbreaking move not only scored the Beatles one of their biggest worldwide hits, but it set new standards for pop songs. The following three years (1969-1971) saw the average length of a #1 song jump to three minutes and twenty-nine seconds, a full 40% longer than the beginning of the pop era. Less than four years after this breakthrough moment, the first #1 hit of 1972 (Don McLean's "American Pie") broke the Beatles' record for the longest #1 single, clocking in at eight minutes and thirty-six seconds.

These breakthrough recordings could have been made earlier than the late 1960s. Any number of artists could have taken those same risks and potentially become successful. Why would all these popular artists stick to rigid formats? For one, they were scared of radio not playing the record. Without radio, you had virtually no chance of sales. This is why only a group as big as the Beatles could leverage their star power for change. But most other artists likely did not think of it. They were safe. Singles, still the primary purchased product, could not get much longer than three minutes. Add all of these elements together and it is clear that the technologies involved in record production and radio distribution set the standards for music production. It did not happen the other way around.

After *Sgt. Pepper's...*, many rock artists expanded the length of their music. The artistic arrangements of *Sgt. Pepper's...* then became more mainstream. And several innovations over a ten-year period allowed more people to hear the album's new possibilities:

- Stereo – The first mainstream stereo recordings came out in the late 1950s, but widespread adoption occurred right around the mid-1960s.
- Powerful PA systems – Live concerts flourished with the new ability to draw enough power to get clear sound out to tens of thousands of people.
- FM Radio – The adoption of stereo on this band in the early 1960s gave this frequency new sonic clarity that was impossible on AM radio.
- New vinyl – Technologies allowed labels to expand beyond fifteen minutes per side in a cheaper fashion that also minimized record breakage.
- Innovations in studio equipment – Master tapes became better, mixing boards got larger, and soon it was possible to create music in several takes, instead of one or two live ones.

This rush of new technologies happened virtually all at once. Without these, the musical innovators of that time would not have flourished as they did. This includes everyone from the Beatles to the Stones, Led Zeppelin to Jethro Tull, and Stevie Wonder to Marvin Gaye. It is fun to mythologize that it was the culture of that time that spawned this creativity: The drugs, the Vietnam War protests, the large population of baby boomers. Those topics are certainly sexier to talk about than new changes in electricity, wiring, and sound waves. But all of that creativity would never have been heard the same way were it not for technology leading the way.

CASSETTES AND CDS

Technology's next big wave came during the record labels' big economic drought of the late 1970s and early 1980s. With the exception of some MIDI and synthesizer innovations, other technologies such as eight-track tapes and quadraphonic sound failed to catch on with consumers. This created even deeper industry doldrums. What saved the industry was another series of technological innovations that occurred over a ten-year period. These led to big booms in the 1990s, because they changed the way people listened to music.

First up was the Sony Walkman. While other portable cassette players were on the market, one brand dominated the marketplace. Cassettes, which were introduced in the 1960s, didn't gain popularity until the 1970s, after technologies like Dolby noise reduction gave the format adequate quality. With the Walkman, you could take music anywhere you wanted. Its ease of simultaneous integration into the emerging fitness trend also helped boost sales.

This device did not only give the burgeoning cassette format success. It also allowed for new maximum lengths in music. Cassettes were thirty minutes in length...sixty minutes... *ninety minutes!* So much more music! Well, much like the LP, it took awhile for song lengths to change. The first cassettes were just regurgitations of the LP, and since the LP was the dominant format, that length determined cassette lengths. It dominated to such a degree that when an LP had sides of two varying lengths (a common concern with the three-minute maximum per song having long been shattered), a warning had to be printed on the cassette stating that the silence was intentional! Cassettes that exceeded the single album length were often record company marketing experiments and repackages. Warner Bros. released a series of "2 for 1" that combined two older albums onto one budget-priced cassette. Island Records experimented with putting an album on one side with no interruption, and then leaving the other side blank for people to add their own music. These were tactics no different than record companies regurgitating singles on new albums in the early days of the LP.

Once again, it took over a decade (until the mid-1980s) before artists started tacking on "bonus tracks" to make use of the expanded length of the cassette. This also dovetailed into the next major technical innovation: The compact disc. This new technology was different in that it offered sound quality that was, by most standards, superior to previous technologies. The crystal clear sound eliminated the crackle in vinyl records and the hiss in cassette tapes. It also allowed the consumer to listen to an entire record from start to finish without flipping over an LP or cassette. And, it gave record labels an excuse to charge more money for a burgeoning new product.

Once again, most CDs released at the time stuck to the forty-five minute mark that was the norm for albums. Like the cassette, the exceptions were repackaging of catalog to show off enhanced features of the CD's capacity for length. A double album on one CD without flipping sides! Complete classical pieces! A greatest hits compilation that can actually fit all the hits!

It was only a matter of time before artists themselves were moved to make longer compact discs. This started in earnest around 1990-1991, only eight or nine years after the technology debuted. Artists such as Guns 'N Roses and Red Hot Chili Peppers released discs with well over an hour's worth of new material, and they were rewarded with multiple hits from these records. A few years later, when Hootie & the Blowfish, Shania Twain, and Alanis Morissette broke sales records with multiple hits, having a megahit album became the rule, instead of the exception.

It also became standard for albums to have well over twelve songs, as opposed to the previous standard of ten songs. The more songs on a record, the more likely one could be a hit. Consumers could also find more perceived value in these releases, as list prices slowly crept up from fifteen to twenty dollars per CD. Marketing costs could be fundamentally lower, as hit albums were promoted for longer than the previous campaign of three to nine months.

CAR STEREOS AND COMMERCIAL RADIO

Throughout the same time period, a slower, subtler change occurred that, at first glance, does not appear to have changed music consumption. Fundamentally, it has. It gave consumers greater choice in their entertainment experience. It also changed the way entertainment broadcasters program their music to generate revenue. This all occurred with the digitization of car stereos.

Digital stereos rapidly revolutionized the way people listened to the radio both at home and in their cars. Prior to the mid-1980s, most people had to tune a radio via a knob or dial that ran across the frequency spectrum. The listener would hope to hit on the exact frequency, and would then usually have to very minutely fine-tune the dial in order to get the exact signal. This process made changing the channel on a radio tuner unwieldy, so most listeners found their favorite station and left the radio positioned there, even if it meant sitting through music they did not like. Radios with analog "memories" for specific stations were too cumbersome to have a significant impact.

In the mid-to-late 1980s, stereos began a rapid conversion to digital programming. The most immediate impact was the digital display that allowed the user to scroll rapidly through the frequencies, and arrive at the exact station much faster than previous methods. Memory buttons also took a giant leap forward. Users no longer had to push a large, manual button. Instead, with a slight touch, they could move rapidly from one frequency to another. The scan button also became very useful in allowing the user to find available stations quickly without spending time utilizing the tuning dial.

The impact on music listening was immediate. Radio station programmers could no longer count on listeners hearing a song from start to finish. With rapid tuning changes, it became common for a user to hear a beginning of a song, decide they did not wish to hear it, and then rapidly change stations. The typical end result was finding a song the listener enjoyed that was already in progress. Since the act of flipping through channels is so rapid, stations had mere seconds to grab the listener.

This new technology required record labels, which relied on radio as their main source for sales, to produce songs that were recognizable in a few seconds. Not just a particular few-second passage, but *any* few-second passage. If the listener could not determine his familiarity and/or enjoyment of the song in that instant, he would not stick around to enjoy the song. Therefore, it would take much longer for the listener to become familiar with that song.

Coupled with that change was an increased reliance on radio callout research to determine which records were popular on air. This is when a ten-to-fifteen-second portion of the song, usually the chorus or "hook," is played for individuals (usually over the phone) to determine their familiarity of a song, and to what degree they like it. While the theories behind this were developed during the 1970s, they became common practice in the 1980s.

The net result was the creation of far more songs with repetitive structures. This is most obvious with sampling, which takes an already familiar song and repeats the recognizable portion multiple times. Songs with this structure have the dual benefit of being familiar from the recycling of the song, along with the repetitive nature of that recycled portion. Other songs just create their own repetitive beat and/or hook, and rely on the catchiness to create enjoyment and the repetitiveness to breed familiarity.

WHERE WE ARE TODAY

Now, in the twenty-first century, the technological changes are familiar, and their impact has been well documented. Napster came on board and caused such an upheaval in the distribution of music that it fundamentally altered the entire music experience. Labels started suing customers for using Napster and the similar services it spawned. Compact Disc sales fell rapidly. The record industry became troubled and beleaguered.

There are so many reasons why the financials fell apart. One big reason is that no company clearly has a financial stake in the new digital formats, like they had in the past. RCA started this business model in 1929 when it merged with Victor so they could make both records and the players they played on. Phillips originally formed a record label after getting into the phonograph business themselves in the 1940s. They then went on to develop the cassette and co-develop the CD, collecting royalties along the way. Sony, the other co-developer of the CD, purchased CBS Records in 1988 so they could also collect money on both ends.

If we are to follow history, it will only be a matter of time before Apple or Microsoft purchases and/or creates a major record label. They are the ones who hold the patents on proprietary Digital Rights Management (DRM), which allows digital music to be enjoyed, but also limits the copies that can be made. However, there is a wrinkle that has prevented this from happening sooner: The only format more popular than AAC (Apple's format) or WMA (Microsoft's format) is MP3, which anyone can adapt and make his own. As record labels began to embrace MP3 in 2008, it will now be difficult to protect any music, much less be able to make money off of a format patent.

This brief dissection of technology's role in music history brings out the cumulative ramifications of where this all is headed, and how it affects the way music is created. Some of it can be learned from previous technological changes and their affect on consumption. Others are garnered from monitoring usage patterns from the growing new ways in which users interact with new music devices. Still others are derived from the business concerns involved in the distribution of music, and how that impacts what music is selectively pushed towards consumers. What history teaches us is that technology has changed the way hit songs are created. Today, it gives us a successful map for the future.

At least until the next technological breakthroughs.

1

IMPACT THE LISTENER
IN THE FIRST
SEVEN SECONDS

You are listening to a song on the radio. The song begins and the DJ is spouting meaningless banter until the vocalist begins singing. You "hear" the song, but in actuality, the DJ is guiding you to the new "beginning" of the song when the singer utters the first note. This is usually fifteen or twenty seconds into the song itself, which sugarcoats the song to the degree that the listener will have heard about thirty seconds before he decides whether he likes it or not. This thirty seconds is not inconsequential, as it is nearly 15% of a 3 1/2 minute song.

When you are dealing with a song that you have already heard, this does not have perceived impact. Most people are already aware of their enjoyment of the song or lack thereof. No amount of enticement from the DJ will affect whether you will tune out.

The real impact of the DJ's "post" of a new song is the familiarity that it can breed over time. Even if the listener does not enjoy the song at that moment, he has heard enough of it to likely respond positively on subsequent plays. As a listener, even if you tune out of the new unfamiliar tune, you have actually allowed 15% of the song to seep into your consciousness. Over time, that will bring familiarity with the song.

This is not the only way that the listening habits of radio cause you to become familiar with songs that were heretofore unknown. With digital radios the norm, flipping through stations full of undesired programming has become an extremely common practice. This then leads to listeners encountering songs already in progress. This can be a few seconds into the song, in the middle, or perhaps the end. No matter where the listener comes in, the chances he will hear a song in a position other than the beginning is very high.

Once again, this holds little consequence to an audience already familiar with a song. Most classic songs have been ingrained so deeply into the audience that any random five-second snippet is likely to elicit familiarity. If this familiarity causes a positive response, the listener will stay with it. If it does not, they are unlikely to change their opinion and stick with the song.

With unfamiliar songs, the reaction can be very different. If the listener hears the middle of the song as his first impression, he is likely to tune out. But that impression is setting up vague familiarity for any subsequent listen. Eventually, through a combination of these "in the middle" impressions, and the impressions over the DJ post (where the listener gets exposed to 15% of the song), the listener will develop familiarity without even realizing it. This can often be achieved over the course of four to seven impressions.

When the listener reaches this point, it is likely he has not actually heard the song in its entirety. However, through the repetitive nature of these impressions, the listener believes he has heard the entire song and feels familiarity. Now, the listener develops his opinion of how much he enjoys the song.

This entire process, while oddly convoluted and difficult to feel in action, is actually very healthy for the music discovery process. Listeners rarely express a desire for new music. In fact, if asked explicitly if they would like new music, most people would not respond favorably. They appreciate it when solid new music "arrives," but that arrival is usually a result of the above process.

Added to the process are the filtering mechanisms employed by radio stations and record labels to limit the amount of new music that actually reaches those ears. Presume for a minute that the average listener has six presets on his radio, all programmed to stations that play new music. (With the proliferation of talk radio and oldies-based formats such as "JACK-FM," this is becoming a less likely scenario.) Each new station "adds," or begins to play, two or three new songs in a given week. With six presets, this would mean the listener has a total maximum pool of eighteen new songs to discover weekly. If you subtract likely duplicates (a new song by a crossover A-list artist is likely to receive airplay on multiple stations), and new songs that get only "overnight" spins, this number will rarely exceed half the pool. So most radio listeners will only have a *chance* of being exposed to nine or ten new songs a week. Since people do other things besides listening to radio, they will usually get exposed to far fewer songs. In today's world, exposure to two or more songs is considered a success. With this very complicated and drawn out process to get new music out to listeners, it becomes clear why it is difficult for people to hear it.

THE DIGITAL REVOLUTION HAS MADE MUSIC DISCOVERY HARDER

The above statement certainly seems counterintuitive. The digital age was *supposed* to make this whole process easier. People were *supposed* to find the songs they want far more quickly than ever. The elimination of radio and record company filters was *supposed* to make the world a fairer place for people to hear songs and make them popular. What happened?

The digital age has made it infinitely easier for people to find, obtain, and experience music with which they are *already* familiar. This familiarity can come from having heard the song previously, or from the knowledge that the song exists. If the listener already knows he is going to enjoy a song, he can easily find it and experience it as much as possible. Since he is already familiar with the song, the choices have mostly been made prior to listening to it. He is either committed to the song or he is not.

For new songs, the proposition is much more dicey. For one, the elimination of filters makes it very difficult for listeners to become familiar with any new songs with regularity. On any given week, between 10,000 and 15,000 songs are introduced through legal digital channels. If you filter out genres that most listeners are unlikely to search through (such as world music and jazz), as well as older songs making their online legal debut, you are still left with several thousand new songs that can presumably be heard for the first time each week. Even with filtering, the universe of new songs is as much as 2,000 times greater than that which had been previously experienced on traditional radio stations.

As radio listenership decreases, the reliance of radio for new music exposure also decreases significantly. As the active music listener gets immersed in the digital age, his primary exposure to new music comes in a variety of ways:

- iPod or other portable digital music player.
- On-demand airplay online.
- Online music video outlets.
- Online radio.
- Mobile music applications.

The majority of these experiences bring with them a certain amount of knowledge about the song. Portable device plays require the user to actively download, purchase, or willingly receive the song, so he must have a prior knowledge of that song. On-demand airplay requires the listener to actively know about that song, and to be looking for it. Same thing for nearly all online music video outlets.

There are some instances where a prior knowledge of the artist is not required, and can result in "pushed" exposure to these new artists. Online radio actually offers a large degree of randomness, as designed by the creators of that station. When you tune in, you will be pushed to a song of their choosing, as well as every song thereafter. You can also get on-demand plays from individual websites when songs start playing as soon as you load the page. While the user has no control over the music (save for muting the song), he does have control over which website he visits, which sometimes has a connection to the music that plays. Social networking sites such as myspace and Facebook also allow opportunities for users to play music upon arrival to an individual's page.

ZERO PLAYS

Throughout all of this, the most common feature of each song's airplay is not the method in which it is distributed. It is not even predicated on whether the airplay is pushed out to the listener, or pulled in from the listener's prior knowledge. All of these things are responsible for getting the song to the user in the first place, but they are not what aids garnering that song a second listen. If you wish a song to be a hit, the second impression is more important than the first. In fact, as stated above, it's really the fifth, sixth, or seventh impression that truly matters.

While online methods have allowed much greater access to a wider selection of new music, this has not changed the major precept of most music listeners. They do not want to hear new music. The subtlety, or lack thereof, that radio employs to expose new music only exists elsewhere in rare circumstances. In most cases, you get one shot at impressing someone with a song. With a wide choice of new music to experience, the listener does not want to waste time on songs that have little to no chance of being enjoyed in the future.

If the listener needs to be snagged from the very first listen, an artist needs to find the most common elements among all music distribution. That allows the listener to get the song, no matter what the situation. This means replicating the experience on everything from an iPod to a personal website, and from major music portals to underground, illegal sites. When you consider all of these experiences both today and in the near future, one common element exists in the overwhelming majority of music plays: The song will start at zero seconds.

To nearly any music listener, this seems obvious and intuitive. This likely also appears banal and so insipid that it should not even merit a mention. All songs start at zero seconds. Everyone always starts listening to the song at the beginning of the song. When people go to a concert, they usually start cheering at the opening chord of a song that they know they are going to love. All of the songs on the CDs a person listens to also start at zero seconds.

But the common thread on all of these zero plays is that they largely occur on songs with which the listener is already familiar. Active music fans may listen to unfamiliar songs rabidly, but the passive consumer who bought a CD for a few hit songs will likely hit the skip button on unfamiliar songs far more often. Over time, the listener might get to enjoy some of these unfamiliar songs. Even then, it is usually initiated passively: The album is played in the background often enough for the unfamiliar to become familiar.

The notion of most songs creating familiarity outside of the zero-second start time has not been widely discussed and theorized. In the timeline of music history, "non-zero" familiarity exposure was barely in its infancy before it began to go away with the rise of the digital age. Historically, songs closest in style to today's modern pop song were mostly played in campfire, choral, or minstrel settings, when the lack of technology prevented music from being widely disseminated and songs were handed down or taught. It is highly unlikely that someone began teaching a song in its middle.

When technology first took hold at the turn of the twentieth century, and recorded music appeared on either single-song cylinders or piano rolls, the mechanics were too cumbersome to suggest that anything but a minute portion of plays began outside of the opening notes. When 78s (and later 45s) came out, single play was also the order of the day, so it was doubtful anyone would jump into the middle of the song unless they already had a high degree of familiarity.

Radio, as it first developed, focused on live broadcasts. The idea of "disc jockeys" did not exist yet. So while there were certainly instances of music being heard with a non-zero play start, most people heard music from listening to scheduled programming. That meant they listened to music from the beginning nearly every time.

The 1950s were likely the first instance where listeners got exposed to a significant amount of music through non-zero airplay. Radio became a world governed by disc jockeys. There was little drama programming, only non-stop music. People would tune in at odd times instead of scheduled ones, which certainly resulted in many non-zero exposures. This exposure, however, was minimal. There were usually very few choices for a music listener on the radio, mostly because there was only an AM band, not AM + FM like today, and there were not necessarily as many stations broadcasting in a given market as in later years. So channel-switching seldom occurred. Similarly, there was no "memory" of favorite stations on the radios, making it difficult for listeners to switch between stations efficiently. As a result, true non-zero effectiveness for new music exposure did not occur on a mass scale until the mid-to-late 1960s with the advent of FM radio, a wider variety of choices, and the initial designs of radios with programmed memory.

That same decade also brought the first mass iterations of the Long Playing record, or "LP," into pop music. Initially, the LP was little more than singles strung together for easy purchase, or the primary format for genres such as classical, jazz or show tunes. In most cases, there was a degree of familiarity that went into purchasing these releases. Since familiarity was key to purchasing the discs, most LPs of popular music featured the famous "hit" single as the first song on the record. This virtually guaranteed that most initial impressions of the album were from the music the listener already knew. It would take until the mid-to-late 1960s for mass ownership of record players that could play LPs. It was then, too, that artists began challenging the structure of the album, and created records that had familiar "hits" embedded deep within the LP, if at all.

Those who grew up with vinyl records have probably grasped how this progression of LPs helped create familiarity of songs through non-zero airplay. In order to access songs not in progression on the album, you would need to physically lift up the needle and place it on the track you wished to play. If you were to play a song exactly at the beginning, you would need to precisely hit the "groove" etched into the record. In most cases, the listener would get the end of the previous song, be placed many seconds into the desired song, or hear some other song entirely, depending on the steadiness of his hand. In other words, he would get non-zero initial exposures to unfamiliar songs all the time. This only increased as albums progressively moved away from hits placed in the opening slot.

HIT SONG INTROS

With so many technological changes in the mid-1960s, the transition then began from listeners becoming familiar with music from non-zero exposure instead of mostly zero plays. This only increased through the modern music era. By looking at the average length of the introductions of #1 songs by year, one can see how this technology shift drastically changed the introductions of popular music.

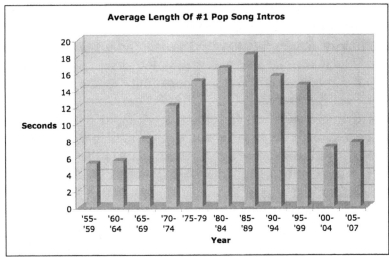

CHART SOURCE: *BILLBOARD/JOEL WHITBURN'S TOP POP SINGLES 1955-2006*

Throughout, some artists created songs purely from their artistic impulses. Others wrote songs to fit radio's criteria in the hopes of making them popular. The trending of song intros shows there was an increase in the length of introductions in popular music as the likelihood of more non-zero music exposures also increased.

The peak of the length of song introductions occurred in the 1980s, when the average #1 song had an intro of 17.4 seconds. This coincides neatly with the rise of the cassette. Where an LP gave the listener a visual groove to attempt to start the song at a correct location, a cassette offered no such luxury. It was even more difficult for the listener to discern where a particular song began or ended to find it efficiently. The estimates listeners employed to find the songs they desired came from their own knowledge of approximate song lengths, divided by their estimates of the speed of the fast-forward and rewind buttons. In other words, they guessed. Naturally, this exponentially increased the number of non-zero plays that existed for people to hear new music.

The 1980s also saw the transition from the analog "memory" of radio stations on car stereos to digital memory. This allowed listeners to effectively switch rapidly between radio stations to find only the songs that interested them. This dramatically increased the amount of non-zero new music exposure. Adding to the likelihood of an increase in station "flipping" was a marked increase in the number of stations playing music that appealed to a wider audience. While FM radio had a significant rise in usage in the 1970s, it was the beginning of the 1980s when both AM and FM became standard on nearly all radios. These changes increased the likelihood that the listener could switch to an appealing choice of music.

The other advent of the 1980s was MTV, which played short-form music video clips nearly every hour of every day. MTV played these clips much like a radio station did, offering a variety of songs book ended by DJs (or VJs) and advertisements. When it was new and fresh in the first half of the 1980s, viewers stayed tuned in for hours on end. Over time, when the novelty began to wane, viewership changed dramatically. In a successful effort to increase ratings and advertising, MTV began the transition to thirty-minute shows, as research and Nielsen reports showed that people tuned in and out often in a fifteen-minute stretch of videos. If they were tuning out that rapidly (presumably because they did not like the video being offered), they would be just as likely to tune back in rapidly when the unpopular video ended. Much like cassettes, users would rely on guesswork as to when that video would be completed. This would certainly result in a large amount of non-zero airplay, either of the song they disliked in the first place (possibly due to unfamiliarity, which could then lead this non-zero airplay to familiarity), or arriving in the middle of a subsequent video. Competition through the 1990s from other channels such as BET and The Box (along with some successful shows such as "Friday Night Videos") only increased the likelihood of channel flipping and non-zero airplay.

None of that should necessarily increase the length of a song intro, but it did. As these non-zero plays increased dramatically, the relevance of the introduction of a song ceased to exist. If many people were enjoying songs in this fashion, then an introduction to a song had little or no bearing on a song's eventual success in the marketplace. Also during this timeframe, callout research – in which a radio station hired a firm to call listeners to ask if they liked a particular song—became refined enough for radio station programmers to use regularly. Since these firms would not have the time in a telephone survey to play someone an entire song, they employed nine to twelve second sections of the song, most often called the "hook." This hook was so crucial that the results of the research could change dramatically, depending on which portion of a song was used. Very seldom was the song intro considered vital enough to be the "hook." In nearly all cases, it was the chorus.

An interesting example of how a song's hook can be spotlighted due to non-zero airplay is in the 1982 Adam Ant hit, "Goody Two Shoes." In this song, the chorus, with the refrain "Don't drink, don't smoke, what do you do?" is repeated incessantly. In fact, it is repeated so often that it takes up 1:08 of a 3:28 song, or nearly 33% of the total running time. In a non-zero environment, this would mean that the listener had a one in three chance of tuning into the "hook," resulting in the development of familiarity. Also, the song has an excessively long introduction, clocking in at thirty-four seconds. As previously noted, a DJ often talked over song introductions, effectively delaying the conscious starting point until the completion of the introduction. If we deduct that intro, the listener actually has a 39% chance of hearing the song's hook, a nearly 20% increase.

The same song in a zero play environment would have a dramatically different effect. For a listener to become familiar with the song, he would first sit through twelve seconds of a relatively generic tribal drumbeat with some acoustic guitar. Then, he would have to patiently wait through an additional twenty-two seconds of instrumental introduction before getting to the first vocals. With these hurdles, the likelihood this song would be a hit in the digital age is extremely slim.

SELECTOR AND INTROS

The length of introductions in the 1990s can theoretically be traced to the necessity of disc jockey banter to include advertising messages. Many listeners have correctly picked up on the dramatic increase in commercials on radio during this time, commonly referred to as "spot load." This was a result of industry consolidation into public companies, and squeezing out more revenue to swell the bottom line. One way that was not so obvious to most listeners was to insert ads into the DJ's talking points before a song began. In order to do this effectively, the DJ needed songs with introductions long enough to get an advertising message across. This resulted in songs with longer introductions getting played more often. These songs would also get played with a DJ introduction, which then would lead to more familiarity as the DJ guided the listener into the song.

But to be fair, radio broadcasters did not program a song just because of its advertising potential. However, the most significant tool in radio programming in the 1990s did this dirty work for them, and the programmer was completely oblivious to the process. How were songs with longer intros programmed without the knowledge of the people in charge? The idea seems preposterous. However, the culprit that made it all happen were computer-scheduling programs, the most common one called "Selector."

What "Selector" does is allow a computer to take a pre-selected list of songs for a particular station, merge them with various criteria assigned to the song, and then spit out a second-by-second playlist of the songs the DJ is supposed to play in that timeframe. No ballads played back-to-back? No problem. At least sixty minutes between songs featuring a particular artist? Easy. Play songs with a specific minimum introduction length at specific points of the day? Done.

So follow this progression of a song with a longer introduction as it gains a competitive edge to becoming a hit. The radio programmer picks all of the songs he wishes to play in a given week. He then decides the approximate range of the number of plays, or spins, that song would receive in that given week, say between fifteen to twenty times a week. If within that group of songs, only one song ("Song A") out of ten had the required length of introduction for particular DJ advertising messages, that song would have a higher likelihood of being chosen by "Selector." This would likely result in the track playing twenty times, while another song ("Song B") that was supposed to receive the same airplay only gets fifteen plays. Five additional plays may not seem like a lot, but the computer has just increased the likelihood of listeners hearing "Song A" over "Song B" by 33%. Now, imagine if this scenario were replicated in twenty or thirty radio stations across the country, all owned by the same company with the same advertising goals. At that point, just by virtue of computer scheduling, "Song A" gets played 100 to 150 times more per week than "Song B," which is supposedly in the same relative sphere of popularity.

Considering the number of radio stations in the country, 100 plays may appear to be minimal. However, the programmers who decide whether these songs should play more often rely on national trade magazines such as *Billboard* and *Radio & Records* (*R&R*), which tally these spins through Broadcast Data Systems (BDS) and MediaBase. These publications and services filter out radio stations that do not fit a particular style of music to create a chart showing the relative success of certain songs in certain genres across the nation. As an example, an Alternative

Rock chart would only include airplay from stations that classify themselves as primarily playing "Alternative Rock" music. In these charts, 150 plays can mean the difference between #32 and #28. It could mean the difference between #22 and #19. Those are minor differences to consumers who often care only about the Top Ten. But to the industry, these differences can be monumental. If "Song B" is stuck at #22 because it cannot get those additional 100 plays, radio programmers across the country could likely view the record as "unsuccessful" and cease playing it. At the same time, with nothing different except "Selector" scheduling, if "Song A" moved up the chart to #19, it would be a Top Twenty record, and the industry would likely say it has "momentum." It does not matter that the momentum was largely generated by scheduling software which fills holes designed to sell incremental advertising dollars. With this "momentum," the same programmers would likely give it a bigger shot by "bumping up" its rotation and increasing the airplay to forty to fifty spins a week. At this point the process can likely repeat.

Do you find this impossible? Then witness the rise of Mariah Carey. In 2005, her success led her to tie Elvis Presley for the most *Billboard* #1 records ever by a solo artist. Something has to be going in her favor, other than her incredible vocal range, stunning good looks, and working with some of the most savvy record label executives, producers, and songwriters at both Sony and Universal. But it turns out that while this power was crucial to give her music prominence, the most important element may have been the abnormally long introductions of her #1 hits. Her timing with the "Selector" effect also allows her to hold the record for the artist with the longest average #1 introduction length in the pop era.

While many song introductions in the 1990s hovered in the sixteen to eighteen second ranges, Carey routinely had song introductions that extended beyond twenty seconds. In fact, two songs ("Dreamlover" and "Fantasy") had intros that neared forty seconds, while "Always Be My Baby" tied for the second-longest introduction of any #1 song in the pop era. (The longest was "Papa Was a Rollin' Stone," by the Temptations, though one could argue the nearly two-minute instrumental intro was actually a true part of the song). Yes, Carey already had a lot going for her, but it was having that little trick up the sleeve that aided her #1 longevity record.

That does not mean that Mariah and her team created the songs with this manipulation of the system in mind. Most likely the idea was *not* part of the creative process. What may have occurred, though, is that someone noticed that Mariah fared better with a longer introduction. From there, consciously or subconsciously, more Mariah songs were created with extended introductions. Many successful music creators get the mechanics of a hit song either by conscious study or through absorption from experience. Yet whereas other innovations occurred with limited, focused distribution points and monitoring outlets, now the distribution is wide and monitoring is difficult at best.

PERSONAL AIRPLAY

Thus, the game begins to change. The non-zero play, which had been taken for granted and never properly quantified, now has shifted back to zero play. The iPod and other portable digital devices eliminated the guesswork that vinyl and cassettes necessitated to find the beginning of a song. The memory size in these players also eliminated the need to keep a large variety of compact discs handy to play in portable CD players. Also, the minute size of MP3 players made them infinitely more portable than similar CD players, which led to a marked increase in popularity from previous portable devices. This has given them far greater market penetration than any previous personal music device.

No matter the size, shape, or storage capacity of these portable digital players, every single play begins at zero seconds. It is currently impossible to start a song file at any midpoint. While one could experience the same playback in all varieties of compact disc players, the crucial difference is the sheer number of songs available at one's disposal. A CD would allow listeners to skip through songs, but only songs that were physically available on that CD. This meant selection was limited and a listener could not receive musical diversity without physically changing the CD. Skipping to different songs was also restricted. With multiple CD changers, a listener could get more musical diversity through song skipping. But even on these devices, skipping was infrequent. Skipping from disc to disc was cumbersome, as it involved the listener sitting through seven to ten seconds of silence as the player manually switched discs.

On iPods, skipping is easy, and even more desired, due to the volume of music contained within the device. As people place thousands of songs on their iPods, they can only know they actually enjoy all the songs thru manual ratings or playlists based on playback information. In fact, people report "discovering" new music within their iPod, as they randomly hear tracks on albums they already have that may not have been readily familiar.

The skip button also experiences increased usage, because the volume of music available means a listener has more choices to find a suitable track, as opposed to limited options on radio or an individual CD. A listener often skips several songs until he actually arrives at a song that suits him at that particular moment. If the listener skips five songs before he arrives at the song he desires, while listening to about four seconds of each song before deciding to skip to another, the whole action would take only twenty seconds, as the skips are instantaneous. It is equally as long with a CD, but the lack of selection would make five skips unlikely. The deeper into the CD one gets, the narrower the selection. On a CD changer, the same process would take nearly a minute, or three times as long. Manually switching out CDs takes even longer than that. The ease and access to diversity has subtly encouraged so much usage of a skip button that musicians need to create with that in mind.

Since there is so little time to ensnare the listener with access to a massive iPod library, he better be engaged immediately. This necessitates a tight and engaging introduction. In many cases, this means exploiting the catchiness of a chorus quickly. Remember that the listener had at least some awareness of the music loaded on his digital player. There is a likely chance that he has already heard the track once, presumably when the track was first obtained. If something needs to trigger a memory of that song from a previous listen, it better be done in those first four seconds. Without that, the song will remain unfamiliar, and therefore be skipped frequently.

This is fine for a personal listening experience, but personal airplay has never been tracked for the pop charts. Pop charts have been assembled by combining single sales at retail with airplay that is created by radio programmers. The chart creators, though, have always wanted the most accurate reflection of the audience's listening habit. If they could have monitored what played on home stereos, they would have. The best they could have achieved that would have been a skewed sampling ala Nielsen television ratings. The charts only tracked actual sales and radio play events because it was impossible to accurately do otherwise.

Today's technology, however, makes this tracking possible. Gracenote was one of the first companies to track this usage, and their website (http://www.gracenote.com/search/charts.php) offers a variety of Top Ten charts similar to those in music trade magazines. The key difference is that these are derived by the music people play on their computer. In most cases, when you put a CD in your computer and the song titles are "magically" displayed, the computer has actually contacted Gracenote's database, which provides the information. Gracenote then tallies this play event. The same thing occurs with music files. With tens of millions of people providing this data weekly, how much longer will it be before it is included in a widely accepted pop chart?

Tracking streams within an accepted site like MySpace or YouTube is easy compared with tracking plays on iPods and any other portable device. How will those plays be tracked? They are not connected to a computer, and there is no WiFi functionality in most popular devices. Active portable device users, however, do sync to their computer often to place new tracks on their iPod, and take off tunes they do not listen to anymore. During this process, it is very simple to also monitor play logs, and iTunes can then provide that information to a chart source such as *Billboard*. Apple made steps in that direction in 2006, when it introduced a new version of iTunes that explicitly collected a tremendous amount of user data. While this caused a minor uproar, and Apple has stated that it uses the data in their store only and then discards it, iPod plays will only become more influential in the future through this data collection.

Another area that is resulting in extensive airplay tracking is with subscription services such as Rhapsody and Napster To Go. In these services, tracking of portable plays is explicit for a multitude of reasons. The services pay royalties to record labels based on each individual play, so they must be tracked to insure proper payments to artists and labels. The services also need to verify that the user is still paying his subscription fee, so devices must sync up at least once every thirty days to ensure that the tracks are active. Without it, the tracks cease to play. With all of this two-way communication on a portable device, a natural leap would be to include these play events in any chart. Now that subscription services are being introduced on mobile devices, their usage will become an increasingly larger portion of daily music usage.

ONLINE RADIO AND SKIP RATES

IPods, despite their deep penetration, are certainly not the only way people have changed the way they get their music. Many people are listening to online radio and watching online video. In April 2008, Edison Media Research reported that 33 million people in the U.S. utilized any number of the legal online radio sites at least once a week. In January 2008, comScore reported that 139 million people streamed online video throughout the month. Within that audience, it is estimated that more than two billion music videos are streamed across all sites every month. That number has only been growing.

At first thought, it seems that these play events should be looked at no differently than traditional music sources. With some sites, this is certainly true. AOL Radio operates under one stream, with multiple users tapping into it. This means that at the moment you "enter" the radio station, you can be placed into any portion of the song, much like turning on traditional radio. However, unlike traditional radio, switching between stations is time consuming, when you take into account the searching, selecting, and buffering of the new signal. While this first song may not be a zero play, the difficulty in switching channels will likely result in that first play being the only one that does not begin at zero seconds.

More online radio outlets actually deliver individual streams, instead of one community stream. This enables the service to create a stream of content that is personalized to the user. The personalized radio services begin all tracks as a zero play, since it is impossible to personalize a stream and at the same time make it available en masse. Many of the most popular services utilize this platform, such as Pandora, Yahoo! Music and Last.fm. These services also offer a popular feature called the skip button. This allows the user, if he is uninterested in a song, to skip ahead to the next one selected on his radio station. It operates in a very similar fashion to the functionality on the iPod. Once again, this guarantees that the listener will get each song as a zero play. In community streams, skipping is impossible. The skip button also, by the nature of its existence, encourages the listener to utilize it extensively. This means if the user is going to be engaged by a song on those radio services, that listener needs to be engaged extremely fast. The success of these sites is only making services with a skip button more plentiful, not less.

Official monitoring of these services by BDS requires that songs play for a minimum of sixty seconds to count as a play. When people use that skip button quickly, the song will not register as an official play. Therefore, these skipped plays will not count toward chart positions, as more Internet music services begin to be counted in national charts. As radio influence diminishes in years to come and digital services gain, this skip button will increase in importance in its ability to make or break a hit. The best way that an artist can avoid the over-utilization of the skip button (aside from making good music in the first place) is to ensnare the listener for at least sixty seconds. Most listeners will hit the skip button within the first seven seconds, making that portion of the song even more crucial. Placing choruses and catchy elements of the song into those first seven seconds is about as much of a surefire approach as one can take to get to that magical sixty-second mark.

Also remember that information provided to these services is a two-way street. That skip button is effective not just at providing a better listening experience. It also gives the service that plays that song valuable data about audience enjoyment. This is something that can be called the "skip rate." If a song is found to have a high skip rate, the service can quickly determine that it is largely unpopular with its user base. If the song is unpopular, the service has little desire to promote it further, as delivering undesired content will likely disrupt loyalty to that service. If a song has a low skip rate, the opposite can occur, and the service may enable the track to play more and become a hit.

As its value increases in these services, and monitored similarly in on-demand audio and video sites, the skip rate can easily make or break a song. The skip rate is akin to a listener switching a radio station. Every radio program director would kill to know what songs cause the listener to press that button and go to another station. In this new paradigm, the online music outlets know which songs cause that reaction. The interesting difference is that the user never switches the station—he just switches the song. In effect, playing a bad song on radio results in a station switch and decreases loyalty. Playing a bad song on the new music services causes a *song* switch and *increases* loyalty. No wonder traditional media is in such trouble!

Traditional radio media will be able to approximate this measurement in the near future, though. The Portable People Meter (or PPM) has begun measuring radio listenership by the second in select cities. The initial uses will be to gauge overall listener tuning hours, and how effectively commercials reach their listeners. Many programmers, though, are already experimenting with utilizing this data to measure the success of specific songs and how much they should be played. It may be a few years before this data is trustworthy and used extensively, but it will have a rapid rise in determining radio programming and will underscore the need for a song to have immediate impact.

For an artist, it is not just the chart positioning and general airplay that remains important. How much the artist gets paid is also something that is dramatically impacted by this technology. Airplay from online and satellite services brings performance royalties that go back to the artist and record label. Knowing that skips occur, some labels are striking deals that allow services to not pay for songs that play only for a short period of time. Thus, potential revenues to the artist will be eliminated simply by a failure to properly engage the listener. Even without these deals, services seeing a high skip rate may limit play, which would have the same net effect on royalty payments. As the royalties from streaming play continue to increase and become an important part of any artist's bottom line, avoiding that dreaded skip button would become a financial necessity.

While this book will offer many more tips on making a song popular, the most important is the fact that the zero play environment is the most crucial industry change of all. Most of what follows will show how to enhance the airplay and increase repeat listenership once people get past that crucial first few seconds. This attribute will be most prevalent in singles, but it will also show up in a majority of an artist's catalog. Without it, those album cuts will have far less appeal and play less often.

Make those first few seconds count. That will be your only shot.

2

LENGTHEN THE SONGS

Traditionally, the pop song has been about short and sweet. Many programmers used to believe the perfect song length was three minutes. Years ago, there were rumors of one radio programmer who challenged himself to take any song and figure out ways to shorten it to three minutes. This would include a masterful bag of tricks such as editing intros and verses, fading endings, and even speeding up certain portions so the song would end quicker.

The truth was that the three-minute rule was mostly a holdover from the average length of a single. There really was no specific rhyme or reason for that figure, other than that was the maximum length a single was technically able to achieve. The first attempt to bring in a single at over three minutes came via the Extended Play single (EP), whereby two songs were placed on one side of a seven-inch record and played at 33 1/3. rpm. The problem was that the sound quality suffered in squeezing these songs on one side of vinyl.

BREAKING THE
THREE-MINUTE STANDARD

A #1 song never truly hammered through the three-minute barrier until 1960, when Marty Robbins broke 4 1/2 minutes with "El Paso." Nobody at the record label thought a song of that length had a chance. To garner airplay, they released a single with a three-minute version of the song. However, the story like nature of the song made the edits awkward and hard to follow, and radio opted for playing the full version. Suddenly, an accepted industry idiom was challenged.

Changes did not fully start until 1964, when The Animals' "The House of the Rising Sun" was released, also with a time of four minutes and thirty seconds. Up until this point, only a couple of longer Ray Charles tracks ("Georgia on My Mind," "I Can't Stop Loving You") broke the three-minute barrier, having sneaked in from large R&B radio success. But these songs took much longer to achieve chart success due to the prejudices against the length. In 1965, the Righteous Brothers exploited that prejudice by outright lying about the total running time of "You've Lost That Loving Feeling." The label on the single claimed the song lasted 3:05, when in fact, the running time was 3:50. By the time DJs realized the ruse, the song had already become too popular to ignore. For the next few years, a small group of #1 songs were longer than three minutes and thirty seconds, but for the most part, songs kept to a length under three minutes. It wasn't until 1968 that the average length of a #1 song finally crossed the three-minute line for the first time in pop history.

Once the public accepted songs over three minutes, singles quickly grew in length throughout the 1970s, when four-minute songs began to be customary. One reason was that seven-inch records could now regularly be pressed to that length by many manufacturing plants. The advent of the twelve-inch single in the 1970s was another. AM Pop radio also started feeling the competition of FM Album Oriented Radio (AOR), which regularly played longer album cuts, such as eight-plus minutes of "Stairway to Heaven," "Paradise by the Dashboard Light" or "Free Bird." Stations also had competition from dance clubs, where songs extended well past the four-minute mark with disco mixes.

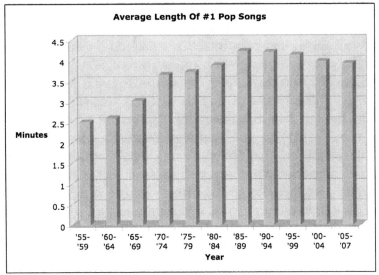

Average Length Of #1 Pop Songs

CHART SOURCE: *BILLBOARD/JOEL WHITBURN'S TOP POP SINGLES 1955-2006*

In response, radio gradually backed off the three-minute rule to remain competitive.

As songs found multiple uses beyond traditional radio play, many other songs also got longer. LPs allowed the artist to create songs that had extraordinary lengths, including many prog-rock opuses in which one song covered fifteen-plus minutes on one entire side. One classic example, Yes's 1974 *Tales from Topographic Oceans,* was a double album with only four songs – one for each vinyl side. Many radio stations started to splice and dice the songs to much shorter lengths. In an effort to maintain quality control (some of these programmers were not good at splicing tape), the artists, producers, and labels took matters into their own hands and edited the songs themselves. While label edits did have an occasional occurrence prior to the 1970s, such as with "El Paso," it was this decade in which the "single edit" became common for radio. Edits also helped radio stations maintain FCC standards, as profanity became socially acceptable on many recordings.

For Top Forty radio, maintaining a short length was crucial. An important tradition in Top Forty radio is the "playing more songs than our competitor," or "more songs in a row," or "X-minutes of non-stop music" rhetoric. The illusion is that the station plays more music than the one across town. The reality is that they still have to sell the same amount of ads as the competition, so the only way to perpetuate the illusion is to keep the songs short. Perhaps these mainstream programmers did not realize that some of these long songs were also partially effective because of the substances consumed by those playing and listening to the music. Then again, given the long-standing payola cliché of "hookers and blow" as a requirement for record companies to secure airplay, they may have been all too aware.

ROYALTIES AND SONG LENGTH

As previously discussed, albums typically contained ten to twelve songs, for a playing time of approximately thirty minutes. The writers of those songs received two cents a song, a rate that was established in 1909 and had never increased. Meanwhile, the price of an LP, which was $3.98 for a mono release and $4.98 for a stereo release through most of the 1950s and 1960s, crept up to $5.98 by the dawn of the 1970s. This meant that on a twelve-song album, only 4% of the revenue made it back to the songwriters.

The band Chicago began to unintentionally change the entire approach to songwriting royalties. Their initial releases in 1970 and 1971 were double albums with song "suites" that could have been viewed as one long song, much like Yes's album in 1974. Instead, they were broken up into movements with different song titles. Here's an example of how this looked on the album *Chicago* (also known as *Chicago II*).

Side II
Wake Up Sunshine
(Ballet for a Girl in Buchannon)
1. Make Me Smile
2. So Much to Say, So Much to Give
3. Anxiety's Moment
4. West Virginia Fantasies
5. Colour My World
6. To Be Free
7. Now More Than Ever

In this example, Chicago would get paid for seven songs that are a part of one long song entitled "Ballet for a Girl In Buchannon." Within that are two hit songs ("Make Me Smile" and "Colour My World"), but they also include five sixty-to-ninety-second largely instrumental passages that blend together. Chicago argued that the suites should not be counted as one song, as slicing them up brought considerable additional revenues to them as songwriters. The end result: The number of songs Chicago got paid on that album jumped from thirteen to twenty-three, a 75% increase in songwriting income.

This same time frame also coincided with psychedelic bands creating extended jams out of one song, and many artists lost revenue opportunities on these recordings. As an example, also in 1971, the Grateful Dead released an eponymous live double record that only had eleven tracks, of which four were covers. That meant Dead-affiliated writers had a pool of fourteen cents per album sold, while at the same time, Chicago collected forty-six cents.

As other artists saw a financial opportunity, the labels quickly moved to close this loophole. In 1972, record companies began instituting a "controlled composition" clause that limited to ten the number of songs they would pay for on an album. A sharp-eyed fan could see the drastic change, as three out of the next four Chicago records contained only ten tracks. One wonders what would have happened creatively had Chicago not been financially restricted in creating these albums. Limiting the songwriter to only twenty cents out of the $5.98 list price was not acceptable, and songwriters and publishers looked to change that. Publishing revenue was often the only way many artists made money when record labels routinely avoided paying royalties on performances.

This is not an insignificant point. Up until the mid-1960s, most recording artists needed publishers to provide them with material, as they were rarely songwriters in their own right. The industry felt most artists were one or the other, but almost never both. With the rise of the Beatles, Bob Dylan, and others as their own songwriters, artists were able to generate more income from their songs, and some labels had an opportunity to save money by cross-collateralizing income. (By combining performance and songwriting royalties into one figure, and deducting expenses on the performance side only, the record label was able to keep a much larger percentage of revenues.) Without cross-collateralization, these artists had at least some income guaranteed by law (albeit two cents a track), which was better than hoping label royalties might show up one day.

The result of the ensuing arguments and Congressional lobbying was a revision of copyright law called the U.S. Copyright Act of 1976. This law established specific mechanical royalty payments for all songs. The royalties were much larger than the previous two cents, and would consistently be revisited (presumably for rate increases) on a regular basis. The basic rate was also defined as any song with a length of five minutes or less. Every song over five minutes earned more money with payments increasing on a per-minute basis.

Remember that the accepted standard for song length through the 1960s was three minutes. Instances where this was broken in the pop world were rare. In the jazz world, songs routinely extended beyond this length. Collecting royalties for songs beyond the standard three minutes was the least of the concerns for black musicians in jazz and R&B. It has been noted that the rise of BMI in the early 1940s was partially attributed to ASCAP's alleged racial discrimination. Other royalties during that period were so rare that it took until 1987, when R&B legend Ruth Brown formed the Rhythm & Blues Foundation, to finally funnel payments to many black artists. So up until the copyright law revision, there was no large industry outcry to even suggest variable payments were needed. The instances where a song extended beyond four minutes were an abnormal occurrence and, as such, did not need to be addressed. And that's where it stands today...sort of.

DIGITAL MUSIC SERVICES

A decade ago, Congress passed the Digital Millennium Copyright Act of 1998 (DMCA). This act established performance royalty payments for digital radio streams. Unlike the 1976 Copyright Act, this royalty paid the artist and not the songwriter. The cost was calculated on individual listens, and figured at a rate of seventy cents per thousand listens. This would equate to either one thousand people hearing a song once at the same time (as on simultaneous Internet radio streams), or one person hearing a song one thousand times (what happens on personalized radio streams). By 2010, this is scheduled to increase nearly threefold to $1.90 per one thousand listens, though Internet broadcasters are challenging this stepped rate increase. As of 2008, the rate is $1.40 per thousand plays, a 100% increase in just three years.

Satellite radio had a rate that was set up similar to the rates set out by the DMCA. However, since XM and Sirius cannot actually monitor the number of listeners of any individual station at any given time, they actually pay on a percentage of revenue royalty. That figure is set at 6% of revenue, which will increase to 8% by 2012. This is then paid out to artists and copyright holders based on the frequency of airplay on these services. As of late 2008, publishers are also being paid similarly for interactive streaming and subscription services, receiving 10.5% of revenues less performance royalties.

These are all important steps toward getting the U.S. in line with the rest of the world. In nearly every other country, artists and labels are paid performance royalties for plays on radio stations, in arenas, etc. The U.S. lagged behind, partially because record sales have traditionally been much lower in other countries than in the U.S. Where a platinum record in the U.S. signifies sales of one million copies, platinum in other large nations ranges from 100,000 to 300,000.

It did not help any arguments for performance royalties when record companies paid radio stations to play their records in the first place. Until Eliot Spitzer, then Attorney General and now disgraced former Governor of New York, came along in 2004, the flow of money was tilting toward radio, and not the labels. As long as the airplay had "promotional value," record sales were plentiful and bigger profits could be had, no one questioned this structure.

Still, with the addition of digital royalties, a rate of $1.40 per thousand listens does not sound like a lot of money in an artist's pocket. If 100,000 people heard a song in a given month, this would bring only $140. Slicing this pie further, SoundExchange, a company set up solely for this royalty, handles most of the collecting. SoundExchange takes 10% off the top for its collection fees before it distributes the rest. The remaining dollars are split evenly between the copyright holder (usually the label) and the musicians on the record. In that math, presuming the collector is one member of a four-piece rock group, that person would receive less than $16. He would barely be able to buy a decent meal at a chain restaurant for the pleasure of 100,000 people hearing his song.

Despite this, traditional radio stations insisted this was a lot of money. Shortly after the law was enacted, nearly every traditional radio station ceased broadcasting its radio signals over the Internet. The primary reason cited by the major broadcast owners was cost. Paying additional royalty costs to the labels just is not in their blood, or their budget. Never mind that, in perspective, costs at that time were not extravagant. Radio stations play approximately 200 songs a day, and around 1999 when all this went full steam ahead, individual stations were lucky if they had a thousand people listening at the same time. This amounted to a whopping $14 a day, given the royalty rate at the time. Of course, stations were more worried about reaching 10,000 or more at any given time. If the Internet audience for major market radio stations reached numbers close to their measured audience on traditional devices, broadcasters could be looking at paying over $500,000 a year in royalties...per station. Multiply that by nearly 1,000 music stations in the Clear Channel network, and that is the figure that frightened the company. (The fact that the American Federation of Television and Radio Artists (AFTRA) demanded additional payments for members' commercial spots made the decision even easier.)

The scale back of terrestrial radio broadcasts on the Internet allowed big Internet-only radio broadcasters such as AOL, Live 365, and Yahoo! to grow substantially. These companies budgeted for radio royalties from day one, and planned their business around it. The virtual Internet silence by terrestrial radio from 2001 until approximately 2004 let these new businesses gain traction. Now traditional radio is struggling to catch up, having lost out on building brand loyalty, and then watching other businesses build cooler features, such as personalization and skipping, that terrestrial radio cannot possibly duplicate.

As the Internet business grows, artists and record labels will rely more and more on streaming radio royalties. In 2006, SoundExchange distributed over $21 million, and that number will grow exponentially with the combined growth in audience and royalty rate increases. In addition to those publicly available numbers, there are plenty more dollars being funneled to record labels, as many record labels are striking private deals directly with bigger content providers. This is done partially to cover changing feature sets that are not covered in the law, including on-demand streaming found on subscription services. A benefit of this shift for labels is the elimination of SoundExchange fees, and a greater ability to cross-collateralize the artist portion of these fees.

Surprisingly, the performance royalty laws and subsequent royalty increases have no mention of time restraints. This seems especially odd given the attention publishers gave to the factor of time in 1976. This means that a ninety-second Chicago song gets paid the same royalty as an eight-minute Meat Loaf opus. The reason could easily have to do with the differences between radio listening and record purchasing. There is technically no lost income if a song is played on a radio service. The artist and label just get the money owed because the song is popular and is played a lot.

Simply examining radio's decision to not enter a space that required them to pay royalties magnifies the flaw in this argument. Even though the royalty payments around 2000 were low, radio did not want to start down that path because of the dramatic cumulative impact on the corporate bottom line. Any one individual song or user is manageable. En masse, it would have meant much more than an inconsequential figure to the bottom line.

AVERAGE ROYALTY PER HOUR

With royalty rates becoming a managed cost, bean counters will look to and attempt to figure out ways to reduce the expense. With song length not a factor, the most obvious way is to look at an "Average Royalty Per Hour" (ARPH). This is a metric whereby a programmer can actually figure out how many dollars are being spent per hour, based on the number of songs being played. Satellite radio argued a variation of this in front of the Copyright Royalty Board in 2007 in an attempt to receive lower rates. The fact that they did not get as low a royalty as they anticipated suggests this practice will be implemented widely as the rates increase.

To show how much can be saved in 2008, let's assume the XM satellite station "Fred" has 1,000 listeners on its AOL radio simulcast at any particular hour. If the station plays fifteen songs an hour (with an average four-minute song), the station will pay $21 per hour in royalties. If the station manages to play twelve songs an hour (with each song averaging five minutes), the station will pay $16.80 per hour in royalties. The programmer has now saved the company $4.20, which is barely anything. However, aggregated out over a period of one year, this simple change would result in nearly $37,000 in savings. Aggregate that on to the approximately seventy stations that play music on XM, and it translates to $2.6 million a year saved in royalties. Remember, that's also only presuming an average of 1,000 listeners. The more listeners, the more those savings pile up, though since XM pays a flat percentage, they would not see the same savings on their satellite end.

One thing to remember—it is not just the songs selected. It is also the ability to lead people to listen to more profitable stations. For example, as previously noted, popular songs through the 1960s were almost always under three minutes. Therefore, it is virtually impossible to put together a 1950s "Oldies" station that has fewer than twenty songs an hour. Meanwhile, when you have ambient and New Age songs that routinely extend well beyond five minutes, it is very easy to have a station that can play fewer than twelve songs an hour.

A natural tendency emerges as the station reduces its ARPH. The outlet becomes incentivized to actively promote that station above other, more costly stations. Some stations cannot avoid being promoted due to their sheer popularity, but this subtle shifting of audience direction towards second tier stations with a low ARPH will help the overall bottom line. Extra, inconspicuous placements of these stations, extra promotional spots on other like-minded satellite stations, and denial of promotional opportunities to other stations are ways that a programmer can help cut costs.

In personalized environments, the programmer must look at the ARPH based on the songs played in relation to the songs skipped in that station. Every time that skip button is utilized potentially increases the royalties the outlet has to pay. Programmers are concerned about high skip rates, for that indicates that the audience is responding negatively to that channel. Programmers are also concerned because their missteps in analyzing skip rates can add a lot of extra cost to the company's bottom line. Unlike terrestrial radio, where poor programming may result in lower ratings, online radio gets doubly penalized with low ratings *and* higher royalty rates.

MIX TAPE MENTALITY

In some genres, this skip rate is unavoidable due to the frame of mind of the people listening, along with the content being created for that genre. This is most notable in the hip-hop genre, where availability of mix tapes, its integrated relationship into the lifestyle, and the tendency to rarely play more than two minutes of any individual song has created a short attention span that permeates all listening experiences. In what we term the "mix tape mentality," these listeners have difficulty listening to songs in this environment for longer than two minutes. For the personalized Internet programmer, this leads to higher ARPH for listeners of hip-hop stations. Could the rise in royalty rates potentially put hip-hop underground as it becomes too costly for mainstream organizations to promote?

This outlook will take additional shape in the next few years when the impact of the Arbitron Personalized People Meter is measured on terrestrial radio stations. Rather than requiring listeners to record the station they listen to in a diary, the PPM will actually measure what radio station they are hearing and for how long. If, presumably, the mix tape mentality is actually found in all forms of hip-hop listening, stations playing that genre will suffer significant declines in ratings, as listeners flip the dial far more often on those stations than on others in the market.

Some of the reasons behind the mix tape mentality have to do with the songs themselves. With many of these songs containing insistent repetition, sixteen-beat loops and few, if any, chord changes, they are best suited for short listening sessions, such as two minutes, or perhaps the ten seconds in traditional callout research. Hip-hop will certainly come under additional examination for this very reason. Artists and producers will need to come up with significant innovations in structure and style to keep the genre relevant in the coming years.

The biggest result of highlighting the loophole of royalties unaffected by duration is that it will likely be closed; though expect that process to take several years. This means that smart music producers will release songs that exploit this opportunity. Quite possibly, independent artists will be the ones most poised to benefit from this loophole. Major record labels still produce music under a "radio ready" approach, which means continuing to limit songs to around four-minutes, among other things. It will be two to three years before a competitive advantage can be exploited. Meanwhile, independent labels and artists are adept at creating and releasing music rapidly. As long as the music is quality, they can realize some extra benefits.

When and if this loophole is closed, royalties will most likely shift to an hourly basis, pro-rated by the songs played within that hour. How this works is rather simple. Assume again that on average fifteen songs are played per hour. This would mean that royalties of 2.1 cents per hour per listener are due at the 2008 rate. The Copyright Arbitration Royalty Panel (CARP) could establish the 2.1 cents per hour rate as a standard, and then royalties would be paid based on how much of that hour a song was heard. In this example, a fifteen-minute song would receive .525 cents, instead of the current rate of .14 cents. That's a nearly quadruple increase in royalties.

If that loophole is, indeed, closed, it will likely put songs on more equal footing. But it only changes the strategy if you are a performer or songwriter. If this change occurs, a programmer will not care about the length of a song, as his cost structure becomes relatively static. The performer, however, will want to take up as much listening time as possible in order to collect larger royalties. Longer songs would simultaneously block other songs from playing at the same time, therefore depriving other artists from royalties. While hardcore music fans (and music creators almost always fall in that category) are more than willing to devote hours on end to listening to music, most people actually have a finite window of time to listen. This might be related to their commute time to and from work (via car or train), the moment they clock in their office, when they take lunch, or when they leave work. It can also mean the time their parents call them for dinner, when a TV show starts, when someone would have to leave for an engagement, or when someone desires to go to sleep.

People do not think of listening sessions as being finite, but they are. Presume a person gets home from school at 4 P.M. and turns on his computer to do homework while simultaneously IMing his friends. He knows that he will be called to dinner at 5:30 P.M. He has ninety minutes to listen to music. At a four-minute average song length, this means he can hear about twenty-two full-length songs during that period. If just one of these songs were double the length, that number would slip to twenty-one. If two songs were around eight minutes in length, the number would slip to twenty. So if an artist created a longer song, he would be able to take advantage of this situation and collect bigger royalties. Yet if an artist felt comfortable sticking to the shorter length, he then ran the risk of losing out to another artist who might craft the longer songs. This is fine if he is one of the other twenty songs chosen in this scenario. But what if his song is supposed to be number twenty-one on that playlist? Or number twenty-two or number twenty-three? The person's time is finite, and the artist could miss out on royalties for no other reason than someone eating dinner.

This would not just make a difference in the royalty structure. It would also affect overall chart positioning. If a longer song keeps shorter songs from being played, it will likely lead to chart growth for that longer song. It may not be enough to produce a #1 pop song that exceeds ten minutes (though anything is possible). But with radio traditionally ignoring songs at these long lengths, any additional exposure to these extended tracks that causes even a slight rise in chart positioning will certainly have a profound effect on the industry.

There is no doubt that the overall quality of the song is the most important element in making sure a song is a hit. Without that, the length is irrelevant. With that in mind, the impact in the first seven seconds gains further gravity. The listener must not skip the song, negating royalties altogether. A skip that occur midway thru the song can be equally as detrimental, if royalties become pro-rated per hour. It would effectively cut that song's royalty in half. Similarly, an eight-minute song cannot be created for the sake of extended length. If it also gets skipped at the two-minute mark, 75% of the potential royalties will go down the drain.

A probable outcome of this is keeping the single as a succinct entrance point for artists. Once fans become engaged in the artist, they can easily explore his catalog much more thoroughly. If they take a liking to that artist, and other tracks in the artist's catalog are a longer length, then the artist can benefit financially in ways other artists could not.

Of course, the trick is to keep that listener far more engaged in the music so he will actually reach those longer lengths. In order to do this, songwriters and producers will likely employ a much bigger bag of techniques to keep a listener hooked longer than he expected. The Mariah Carey trick of a longer introduction is no longer viable. If anything, everyone must dive into the body of the song to create new, subtle ways to increase listening time at any length.

3

INCREASE CHORD

CHANGES

This is the part of the book where traditional songwriters will likely raise a big cheer, and with good reason. In pop music, chord changes have been nearly wiped off the face of the earth. Hip-hop producers more interested in the right "groove" than the "song" have created tunes that are basically the same chord repeated over and over. Not even the same chord progression...the same chord. Producers pick a sample or rhythm loop, take one chord (or a simple two-chord progression) from that sample or loop, and repeat it over and over throughout the four-minute length of the song. It has not occurred in every song, but it has dominated enough that it can be identified as a trend from the late 1990s through the 2000s.

Before we analyze why this will not work in the long haul, we have to understand why it *has* worked in recent years, mostly through the sample. While some sample uses were artistic and challenged traditional ideas of a song, they were initially avoided by major labels for fear of the unknown and what that could do to the bottom line. For example, the first song that set some boundaries was the Sugarhill Gang's "Rapper's Delight," which sampled a Chic song throughout while the group rapped over the sample.

The group failed to get permission for this, and Chic ended up with all the songwriting royalties. That left the group with only one hit, and one that provided much less income to the group itself.

Up until the end of 1991, sampling on records had very little legal precedence, despite having been prevalent in urban music for over a decade. Then, in December 1991, Biz Markie and Warner Bros. Records lost a lawsuit brought by Grand Upright Music, which owned the copyright to a sample that Markie had used. Overnight, paying for samples became mandatory. While this brought the use of multiple samples in a song down to one in most cases, it also brought much needed structure to the business of sample clearances. By business necessity, having the budget for only one sample or interpolation included in each song helped solidify a one-groove mentality.

With issues regarding sampling straightened out, a regular process was established that allowed standard treatment of royalties for performance and songwriting (though the dollar figures could swing wildly). This set the stage for many songs to feature sampling as a primary portion of the song. This sampling was also implemented for familiarity. By engaging the listener with a portion of another song that is already familiar, artists might easily lead that listener to gravitate to the newly recorded work. Hip-hop artists most often did this, but R&B singers also reinvented samples. This familiarity led people to be more apt to enjoy the song on the radio and purchase the song, as well.

SAMPLES AND CALL-OUT RESEARCH

A side effect was the new song's ability to score high in call-out research. Call-out research determines which songs stay on playlists of many radio stations. By having a song based on a sample, these songs routinely scored higher on "familiarity," something radio programmers love to see.

This causes programmers to play the songs more, which of course, breeds higher familiarity. Ultimately, it's uncertain whether the newly recorded song was actually the familiar part, or if it was the sample. Eventually it did not matter, as these songs gained high radio airplay and sales, thereby validating a successful approach to making a hit.

This rise in sampling, as well as call-out research, came as radios with digital tuners reached full-market penetration. In the mid-1980s, switching radio stations instantaneously without punching a big button was still a fun new novelty. Car stereos with digital tuners and CD or cassette decks were hot target for theft. By the early 1990s, it was practically ubiquitous in all car stereos. Radio consultants were finding that it was getting more difficult to keep people tuned into radio stations.

Uses of obvious samples appeared to be a fantastic solution for radio stations to retain an audience and avoid the channel flipping from digital tuners. The real key to hold the listener, however, was the monotony of the sample itself. By having it repeat every sixteen beats or sixteen bars, the sample was repeated within a five to twenty-five second period. In other words, it was repeated so often that you were virtually guaranteed to hear the familiar hook at just about any point you tuned into the song. This attribute was a crucial element to achieving that increasingly elusive tune-in.

The downside of songs with heavy sample use was masked for the better part of the decade. Because ratings, research, and sales were so large, no one asked the difficult questions, such as how this sampling might meld with the mix tape mentality mentioned in the previous chapter. The fact that large portions of the audience regularly listen to mix tapes (or mix shows on these same radio stations) that cut these songs down to two minutes reinforces that mentality. The audience expects the song to be short, especially given the short attention span of many people today. As such, another factor comes in when that same audience listens to the whole song: Boredom.

CALL-OUT RESEARCH AND NEW COKE

In many ways, business decisions made from call-out research data is about as fiscally savvy as the introduction of New Coke in the 1980s. The fact that New Coke was a huge fiasco for Coca-Cola has been well established. The question that often gets overlooked is how such a large company could make such a huge mistake. Surely the company did extensive research and testing prior to bringing the product to market.

In fact, it did. While many business theories were considered, mostly around the tampering of a beloved brand, a far different theory emerged from market testing data. In his book, *Blink,* Malcolm Gladwell details the flaws in Coke's methodologies, called "sip tests." Coke asked users to drink some New Coke and give them their thoughts. They took a sip and determined that it had a very pleasant taste. When this result became fairly common, the company went forward on producing the product. Of course, it failed to test someone drinking an entire glass or can of New Coke. When the product was finally released, consumers found that the first sip was pleasant (as shown in testing), but by the fifth or sixth sip, the taste resulted in a very negative experience, which led to the soda's demise. Coca-Cola had failed to replicate full consumer usage in its testing.

Despite such a notable failure, radio stations and record companies continually use this same type of methodology to determine which songs should be hits. They offer consumers "sips," or seven-to-ten second bites of the song's hook, and ask them to judge that portion of the song. The cost of testing an entire song (let alone dozens of songs) is just too expensive, and people do not have the time to sit through such testing. In that regard, the decisions made on which songs become hits are never predicated on how people actually hear the music. Instead, radio stations and record companies routinely throw up research with as much validity as New Coke had, and then scratch their heads when these supposed "hits" don't sell or drive radio ratings higher.

In zero play environments, all of the audience hears the song from the beginning. With songs that contain a notable sample, the beginning is usually the point that the sample is clearest. This is actually a double-edged sword for that seven-second rule. The positive angle is that in the early stages of the song, the instant familiarity causes the listener to stay tuned for a large chunk of the song. The negative side is that the overly repetitive nature of the sample causes many users to lose interest, usually about two minutes in, when the second chorus completes.

By repeating the sample over and over, the listener finds the full song uninteresting and boring. Every once in awhile, he may want that "taste," but increasingly it becomes harder to get him to listen to the whole thing. Additionally, the very use of the sample causes these songs to be more of a "foreground" experience instead of a "background" one, thereby increasing the likelihood the song will not be a long term hit. (See more on foreground vs. background in Chapter Eleven.) If the artist wants to make money off of these songs in the digital age, the song cannot be monotonous. This is especially important with songs that contain samples, as the royalties have to be split with the owners of the sample.

Nowhere is this shift more apparent than in the sales chart. In the top ten digital downloads for every year since 2005, only one song has contained an active sample (Kanye West's "Gold Digger" and "Stronger," and Shakira's "Hips Don't Lie"). Likewise, on the top ten album sales chart, three of the top albums in 2005 relied on active sampling (50 Cent, Kanye and the Game). None appeared in the top ten in 2006, and only one (Kanye) appeared in 2007.

A song cannot rely on a monotonous, sampled groove in order to be hit worthy. It helps to explain the popularity of Gorillaz' "Feel Good Inc." in 2005. At first listen, while it did not contain a recognizable sample, it did have a monotonous sampled loop at the beginning (which actually had one chord change in it). Eventually, this loop enabled it to establish good numbers in call-out research that made radio comfortable to play it. Listening to the whole song, however, you hear the styles changing rapidly throughout the song. One second it is electronic dance music, then it becomes rap, then it is almost rock, then it goes…well, just about everywhere. This constant shift in styles was a major contributor to the song's popularity. The results were a top ten song in nine countries and the thirteenth biggest-selling download in 2005, ahead of much bigger chart hits.

Most artists will not be adept enough, or carry the personnel, to pull off the genre shifting that Gorillaz did. The simpler way to arrive at similar results is to add chord changes throughout the song. This can be done in a variety of ways. It can occur during the verses, the bridge, or even an instrumental section right around that two-minute "boredom" mark. That way, the song can draw the listener back in just when he was ready to throw in the towel. There can also be a big key change in the chorus toward the end of the song. Remember when those were in nearly every chart-topping hit? They are going to be more crucial in the future.

"CHORD CHANGES" IN OTHER MEDIA

Other media formats are already adopting similar changes to keep their audiences engaged. Perhaps the most successful use of the formula is the TV show "24," which uses the narrative device of taking place in real time over twenty-four hour-long episodes in a twenty-four hour period. The assumption has been that by having each episode end in a cliffhanging plot twist, the audience keeps coming back for more. Equally compelling in keeping people tuned in is the multiple story lines and the ticking clock, omnipresent throughout the show's hour. The viewer is rarely given more than three minutes with any one aspect of the storyline, which keeps him interested and prevents boredom.

Perhaps this also led to the surprise success of the movie *Night at the Museum.* In the movie, Ben Stiller gets a job as a night guard at the Museum Of Natural History, where the dioramas come to life. While Ben Stiller's character, Larry Daley, was the anchor thread throughout the film, the actual movie contained multiple characters and plotlines to which the filmmaker kept returning. This included:

- Larry's relationship with his son and ex-wife.
- Larry's relationship with the museum curator.
- Larry's efforts to thwart the old museum guards.
- Larry's efforts to avoid being fired.
- Larry's exploration as to why the museum came to life.
- Larry being antagonized by a monkey.
- Larry making a dinosaur happy.
- Larry's keeping the peace between Octavius and Jedediah.
- Larry's arrangement of a romance between Teddy Roosevelt and Sacajawea.
- Larry's avoidance of a clash with a hoard of Huns.
- Larry's taunting by an Easter Island statue.

With a running time of 108 minutes, this means each of the above storylines received an average of around nine minutes apiece. By constantly moving from storyline to storyline, not to mention integration of several other characters, the audience, made up primarily of children and tweens, is fully engaged throughout. Much like many chord, instrument and/or style changes keeping a song listener engaged, these constant changes in the movie contributed to its highly successful box-office run.

The important thing for a song creator is to remember to make those changes. Just altering portions of the song will not be enough. Lest urban music seem especially singled out in this regard, rock is also at risk. By the nature of the genre, it is easier to shift creatively in this environment. Take, for example, the standard three-chord rock/blues number popularized throughout the 1950s, such as Elvis Presley's "Hound Dog." Many artists found this to consistently be a reliable structure on which to base hit songs, even in recent years. This holds true…if your song lasts three minutes or less. Those chord changes also become monotonous. To achieve the chart and financial successes a longer song will likely afford, there had better be some change-ups to keep listeners interested.

In recent years, mostly due to callout research, many rock artists find themselves recording with that sixteen-bar loop mentality that the urban artists have mastered. This will be increasingly harder to maintain with digital platforms. Just because rock listeners do not consume mix tapes as avidly as hip-hop fans does not mean the boredom of repetitive loops will not adversely affect the listenership of those song. They also tend to have a shorter shelf life than rock songs of earlier eras. As with past formats within the music industry, catalog "sales" have been a vital component for both the label and the artists. Without a catalog, an artist will enter his later years without a steady income, which results in many artists living out their final years in near poverty. The sixteen-bar loop songs of recent years, due to boredom that sets in through the length of the song, hold less weight and become much less valuable. Artists interested in having a career that pays dividends for decades to come are wise to embrace chord changes quickly.

FUTURE CHANGES

A significant trend in the next few years will be the rise of chord-changing bridges after the second chorus. This technique has been used in many songs in the past, but with the change in listening habits it will become much more common. It also can fit in with continuous groove productions that have become popular in the last decade. At the precise moment when the listener might get bored (at approximately two minutes in), the chord shift would occur and the listener will remain engaged.

There will also be a return to key changes in the final chorus. These can make a monotonous song more interesting, and allow the listener enough diversity to listen to completion. This was used to perfect effect in Sisqo's 2000 hit, "Thong Song." As the need to retain listeners past the four-minute mark becomes more vital for charts and royalties, the end chorus key change is just the technique that keeps people listening longer.

As audiences get accustomed to these transitions, and their implementation becomes a requirement for success, groove-based songs will be minimized and certain genres will experience wholesale shifts in song popularity. Artists that have more traditional R&B structuring will be more successful than in the past, as witnessed by the rise of Alicia Keys in recent years. In rock, the seeds are already there, and are just waiting for the right songs to pop. The emo genre, which originated in hardcore punk, has been steadily increasing in popularity, and much of that is likely because it is the first new rock offshoot in many years to regularly use this technique. Artists are placing multiple chord changes in songs more often in this genre, which appeals mostly to an audience that is completely digitally wired. This is reflected by strong online activity, but smaller physical sales and a lack of presence atop traditional sales and radio charts.

Another group of artists who are also very experimental with chord changes are avant-garde outsiders such as the Arcade Fire and the Decemberists. These artists are following art-rock traditionalists such as Talking Heads by spending several years building up solid fan bases that stick with them for many years. Eventually, they pop into the mainstream, much like Talking Heads did with "Burning Down The House" in 1983. (It never made them pop stars, but it certainly cemented their success.) As bands in this style improve their songwriting, there is a probability that one of their songs will connect so well to this audience base that it will become a huge hit in the new digital environment. Unlike many pop music producers of the moment, their comfort with unique chord changes have them poised for this in a very significant way.

Country music will also grow in popularity, which historically happens at a time of any major sea change in music. The early country movement of the 1950s occurred right at the same time as the birth of rock 'n' roll. Several artists, such as Elvis and the Everly Brothers, deftly crossed into both worlds. The next big wave occurred with soft AM pop in the late 1970s, as country artists such as Kenny Rogers and Crystal Gayle recorded songs that fit well with multiple music formats. The big explosion of Garth Brooks and the 1990s country artists occurred with two significant changes in the music industry: Grunge music and SoundScan. By providing an antithesis to the harsh sounds of the growing rock movement, *and* by having a tallying service that accurately measured the genre's popularity, country music again came back to the forefront.

The next wave is about to happen, and it is no coincidence it is occurring with the digital sea change. The seeds are already sown with artists like Taylor Swift, Keith Urban, and Dierks Bentley, who show a willingness to reach for audiences outside of Nashville. With digital discovery bringing down musical format barriers set up by radio, these artists recognize that the recipe for success means actively working to reach fans outside of core country music. (More on that in Chapter Eight). Most importantly, they are providing chord changes that sound familiar to country audiences, but are also new and fresh to other listeners who have not heard many chord changes in their recent hits. Country's popularity might actually grow faster if pop and rock artists do not embrace chord changes quickly. Its natural ability to work with chord changes, something that it never moved away from, makes it naturally suited to prosper with the digital explosion. The only reason a listener might be bored is because his tastes stray way left of country music in the first place.

There are likely many ways in which the chord change will manifest itself over the next few years. As users gain more control of the songs delivered to them, there is no doubt these sounds will be both plentiful and interesting. With little need for callout research and channel flipping, all of the elements within a hit song have to get more unique, not less, and chord changes will be the first element artists will experiment with and change. Another technique is just as compelling, and will follow close behind.

4

MAGNIFY THE USE OF

DYNAMIC RANGE

A common complaint about radio is that it feels very flat, and this sentiment does not come by accident. Conventional wisdom of radio programmers keeps the sound of an individual station "consistent," so people will not tune out. There is a certain amount of truth to this wisdom. Many people want a music experience that does not vary. While the ability to change channels and songs is much easier than ever before, most people would prefer to never make a single change. They want the music to remain in the background as they go about their daily activities.

Club culture has also grown substantially in recent years, and predictably that environment also wants a relatively flat sound. You need to keep the dance floor moving "consistently" (there's that word again!) so people perspire. When people sweat, they drink, connect with the opposite sex, and – club owners hope – associate the club with that sexual energy so they return to repeat the experience. In order to achieve that, the DJ must beat-mix songs to perpetuate that vibe. Translation: Music must be consistent.

With radio and club play driving awareness, charts and sales, there is little reason for artists to make changes. Creating music that has a flat, consistent sound from beginning to end still yields the most overall success. While digital platforms offer much more musical variety, the radio stations that provide a flat, background experience always perform extremely well. Online hype may lean toward indie rock music, but heavier traffic tends to go to stations such as "Lite Office Music," "Beethoven.com," and XM's "The Heart." It is also very important that most people's iPods replicate a consistent experience.

So why would dynamic range actually be important in the digital future? One might think that with all of these popular flat platforms being used regularly, an artist breaking from that mold might have trouble finding an audience. In truth, the digital environment actually affords those artists opportunities that never existed before. In turn, these songs are much more likely to bear commercial and financial fruit.

FRESH DYNAMICS

In previous years, virtually the only way for a song to get mass exposure was through radio and music television. It has been quite some time since these outlets openly embraced music that contains a variety of dynamic ranges. That kind of music has occasionally existed, but producers at major labels have largely steered artists away from it. Conventional wisdom dictated that those songs would not get played, and therefore never sell. Dynamic music just never had a chance, no matter which way you slice it.

In the digital environment, dynamic range will sound so fresh to tastemakers that songs that exhibit it will likely be played more often. These songs will also be the ones more likely to spread virally by these same tastemakers. This will spawn some royalties for the artist. But it will be no guarantee of chart positioning to help grow that success, so freshness alone will not make this a likely trend in popular music. The successful underpinning of dynamics in a song is the subtle manipulation of the listener. The goal: To get him to listen longer.

Dynamics can be used in too many different ways to chronicle here. But the successful use of dynamics coupled with the digital technology that allows artists to do things that were not possible a few years ago will result in exciting new techniques. In all of the usages, dynamics will be placed strategically in nearly every second of a song, and subconsciously bring the listener into a longer engagement with the music.

Take the beginning of a song. Perhaps a long fade-up can convince people to stick around for the first thirty seconds, as the song would be unlikely to truly "start" before then. If deployed properly, that song would be thirty seconds ahead of every other song in total length. It would also likely extend the time before someone hits the dreaded "skip" button, thereby giving the song an advantage in growing royalties and chart position.

Think that will not work? It certainly can, and was even successful in the pre-digital era with "The Reflex" by Duran Duran. This song started with a fifteen-second fade up that referenced the chorus of the song and helped draw in the listener. This technique allowed the band to have its first #1 record in the United States, making it bigger than other memorable hits such as "Hungry Like the Wolf" and "Rio." Also, at 4:26, the song was the longest #1 song of 1984, in a year where nearly every other #1 song hit the four-minute mark with exact precision. So now, in this new digital age, which song would make the most royalties in a "#1 Hits of 1984" playlist?

THE BUILD UP

Building up to a big chorus is also another tradition in pop that will likely make a more significant comeback in the near future. With the exception of some urban songs, this never really went away. Producers and artists have known for years that the chorus "sells" the song, so they downplay everything before this point in the song in order to make sure the chorus stands out more. This includes scaling back the drums, withholding guitars, and doubling the vocals at the chorus to make the voice sound bigger than life. Subtle tweaking of the mix to make sure the chorus is actually dynamically louder than the rest of the song also often occurs.

The sonic buildup in the digital environment is also important because most casual users want to stick with a song if they think something important is going to happen. Think of it as the equivalent of a newscast which teases with "a crazy car chase on the freeway that you don't want to miss." (Which, of course, will be after the commercial.) You know the chase will be lame. You know it is nothing you have not seen before. You also know that wanting to see what today's definition of "crazy car chase" is will keep you hooked those extra few minutes.

Dynamic buildups in the beginning of a song operate in much the same way. Listeners have been trained for years that those natural buildups lead to something, and that they are worth waiting for. If that dynamic range is not offered and the listener is not interested in the song, he will leave very quickly. If there is something mildly interesting going on in that early soft dynamic portion of the song, he will want to stick around for the payoff. Then the artist has the listener in the palm of his hands. The crafty producer will then make sure that the "payoff" occurs at any point after sixty seconds. This, of course, will insure a play monitored by chart services, along with royalties that would far exceed those made from seven seconds, had the dynamic range not been implemented.

These buildups are also a traditional way of getting listeners interested in songs from genres that might be considered too harsh or foreign for the average listener. In 2003, the song "Seven Nation Army" by the White Stripes became a big success and catapulted the band to mainstream notoriety and platinum sales. Certainly the strong hook of the instrumental guitar line helped out. But what really enabled the song to score with listeners was the dramatic buildup. Many casual listeners turned off the White Stripes' many earlier and subsequent singles, such as "Fell in Love with a Girl," because their trademark fuzzy guitar started right from the beginning. Even strong hooks could not save it if listeners were turned off by the initial sounds. By bringing in that subtle buildup in "Seven Nation Army," they had a song that will be played for many years to come. Since the White Stripes are better known for fuzzy guitars than dramatic buildups, it is highly likely that most casual music fans will look back on the group as a one-hit wonder, despite their popularity among indie tastemakers and critical cognoscenti.

MOMENTS OF QUIET

Quieter moments in a song's middle section (again, around the two-minute mark) will likely have a much bigger presence in the future hit song. Chord changes, as the last chapter explored, will also be effective at this point in a song. But as many songwriters know, a song may not naturally flow to a particular technique just because one wants it there. So a suitable alternative will be to create any number of methods to drop the dynamic levels at this strategic point. Among the techniques that can be employed include a complete drop-out of sound, removal of key instrumentation, as well as a slow trail-off of the final chords of the chorus as they lead into solo instrumentation.

The quiet middle and the initial dynamic buildup never really disappeared in rock songs. They did, however, diminish, and their practice will likely return with more regularity in the coming years. Where the practice will noticeably show up is in urban genres. The most obvious hit rap song with a buildup is Grandmaster Flash and the Furious Five's "White Lines." Other examples in hip-hop are few and far between, and perhaps the lack of execution of this technique may explain the genre's decline in recent years. In order to remain competitive, all genres that have gravitated to flat dynamics in recent years will have to start adopting sharp dynamics regularly, or they will find themselves shut out of the charts.

THE FINISH

The ending of the song will also see many manipulations of the fade in order to hold the listener a few more seconds. By this point, if the listener has not actually skipped the song, he is unlikely to do so unless the ending is overly long. Manipulating a fade so that it lasts sixty seconds is not the approach producers should take. However, a fade that was originally set to last fifteen seconds could easily extend to twenty-five or thirty seconds. In the past, these considerations were usually self-censored in the studio for radio purposes. A prolonged fade was not something many did, as it would be the first thing edited for radio play.

In the scheme of things, audiences will not warm to the idea of prolonged fades if explicitly presented. This is largely a subtle manipulation to generate a few more royalty dollars. How many dollars? If eight songs in the artist's catalog are extended an additional fifteen seconds, that would produce an extra two minutes of listening time. This might amount to an additional 3%, which hardly seems worth the trouble. This additional 3% for a hit artist, however, can likely add up to hundreds of thousands of dollars when all income streams are considered. Even a non-hit artist can see several thousand incremental dollars in royalties. In the publishing world, an additional fifteen-second fade can increase a song from 4:46 to 5:01, taking it over the five-minute mark.

The long-fade technique of dynamic manipulation will only prove to be financially effective once royalties move to an hourly rate, or some other form where song length affects royalty payments. Until then, smart programmers may program that song more frequently, simply because it is longer than other songs and helps keep down their ARPH.

There is another subtle manipulation that can be added to a song ending that can drive up royalties. When people purchase an album, or radio plays a song with this technique, it usually does not reap additional benefits, other than getting people to like the song. In the new digital reality, this technique will be repeated far more frequently, simply because it will mean higher royalties and likely make it a hit song faster. In fact, as you are about to see, it may change the speed in which songs get to the top of the chart.

5

MANIPULATE SONGS WITH FALSE OR INCOMPLETE ENDINGS

"Wannabe," by the Spice Girls, is arguably the best pop song ever written, and certainly one of the most successful of the 1990s. At 2:53, it fits the definition of the perfect three-minute pop song almost to a "T." Every step of the way, the song manipulates the audience into having no choice but enjoy the song and listen to it over and over. After brief sound effects of footsteps and laughter (to allow for an allusion to the music video), the song starts out with a big "Yoooooo" clarion call that immediately draws the listener's attention. Lyrically, Mel B proceeds to say that she is gonna "tell you what I want," and establishes what would become a bridge into a full-fledged B-level chorus in its own right. Addressing the audience is about as engaging as it gets. Then the actual chorus comes where the girls explicitly call out, "If you wannabe my lover/You gotta get with my friends." They continually address the listener, telling him exactly what to do, and they do it in a chorus that is pure pop perfection. That they "wanna zig-a-zig-ah" is just that extra "spice" (pun intended) that makes it different.

The real selling point, however, is the way the length ties in succinctly to the song's ending. In 1997, by the time the song went #1 in ten countries including the United States, "Wannabe" was the shortest #1 song of that year. No other song was under three minutes and, unlike 1984 when "The Reflex" was #1, many songs extended into 4 1/2 minutes. This position might have had the song get lost in a sea of songs that dominated more time on the airwaves.

The secret weapon was the ending. The song *felt* like it should have been a 3 1/2 to 4-minute pop song, just like every other hit at that time. To create that feeling, the producers cut the song at the knees. The last thing heard in the song is the a cappella line, "If you wannabe my lover," which is also the first lyric of the chorus. This manipulation is very similar to the slow dynamic buildup at a song's intro. The audience has a natural desire to hear something to its completion. When they expect a song to go somewhere, they will not feel completely settled until that song resolves itself. "Wannabe" never resolves, and therefore creates a situation where the listener cannot get the song out of his head.

THE SONG STUCK IN YOUR HEAD

Everyone has had that experience – a song will not leave your mind for several hours, if not an entire day, and you have no idea why that particular song remains lodged in your memory. In most instances, to attempt a resolve that the listener never hears, the brain will replay the song over and over until it can mentally come up with a resolution.

In 2005, as reported in the journal "Nature," a team from Dartmouth College indirectly examined this phenomenon. They found that when they eliminated sections of songs, people ended up mentally filling in the silent gaps, thinking they heard music when none actually played. The portion of the brain called the auditory cortex remains active, even though music ceases. Lyrical portions are also much more likely to remain active, as they do not rely on the advance sections of this area of the brain.

The partial listen that necessitates the brain to fill in the gaps and resolve can occur in multiple ways. It can come when a listener reaches a destination and turns off his iPod or radio. It can occur when someone leaves a store with a song unfinished in the background. It can even come from a popular song being partially played in a movie or advertisement. No matter how it occurs, the lack of resolution causes that song to remain in the listener's mind, and gives either a false sense of the song's popularity or becomes a nagging nuisance.

Modern pop songs that revolve around a sample and/or song loop have done themselves a long-term disservice. With a closed loop, the song essentially gives the listener a continuous resolution. There is a markedly reduced chance that a listener will leave the song incomplete, at least in his mind. Unlike pop songs with chord changes that often only fully resolve after each chorus, the looped pop song is resolving itself throughout the song, potentially even dozens of times.

In this regard, "Wannabe" had a perfect unresolved ending that demanded repeat listening, as the ending was the beginning of the chorus, not the end. This caused the listener to desire hearing the entire chorus again. If he did not hear it, the listener would likely have the unresolved refrain stuck in his head whether he liked it or not. By a show of hands, have you had "Wannabe" unwittingly lodged in your brain, even if you have always detested that style of music? Do you have it stuck in your head now?

Adding to the lack of resolution is the lyric itself. What do they have to do if the listener wants to be her lover? Yes, you heard the response previously. But much like a trivia question to which you already know the answer, the natural response is to wait until the answer is given. Proving you know the answer reinforces confidence and is a very natural instinct. In that regard, the listener will mentally complete the lyric, but will not feel at ease until the singer who is supposed to complete the lyric actually does so.

The figurative cherry on top is the a cappella ending. In most songs, the instrumental arrangement resolves the song, not the singer. Think of "Let It Be," by the Beatles. Even after Paul McCartney completes the lyrics, the song still does not feel finished until the organ reaches that final C chord at the end. Having the arrangement reach that point is a significant indicator to the listener that the song is complete. By the producers of "Wannabe" adding this technique on top of all the other pop manipulation, they provide the recipe for a flawless pop song.

Through these techniques, "Wannabe" was propelled to #1, created multiple platinum awards, and earned a lot of money for all involved. Yet is it possible that it could have made even *more* money? If it had been released in the new digital paradigm, the answer would almost certainly be yes. The sales would have still been there to the degree they were. The key difference is found in the streaming royalties it would have collected.

MUSIC'S MOEBIUS STRIP

As songs and videos are available on demand and royalties are collected through these plays, any song that results in repeat plays will benefit greatly. When a song is heard that causes the listener to respond so positively that he has to hear it again, he can now immediately do so. Nearly every song can experience this, but a rare few will actually have this occur on a mass scale. By manipulating the ending of the song, "Wannabe" quickly becomes one of those songs. It actually becomes even more effective, as the song will never resolve. No matter how many times you listen to it, those lyrics and chords will never kick in at the end. This will likely result in many listeners playing it four...five...who knows how many times in a row? You will want to get it out of your head, but you will not be able to do so.

In the mid-1990s, when radio and video channels were the only outlets that the song could be heard on, a listener had to buy the record to repeat the song ad nauseum. But it took time to get to the store and purchase it, and once you have that magical song, you want to hear it multiple times. Immediately! This is likely why one of the first places "Wannabe" broke in both the United States and England was on the video channel The Box. On that channel, viewers could call a number and request the video to play and play again. At its height of popularity in the United Kingdom, "Wannabe" was reported to have played as many as six times an hour. The fact that the Spice Girls were attractive women only enhanced that repeatability of the video.

YouTube has now emerged as an even more effective platform for an artist to reap the benefits of this technique. Like The Box, once a user watches a video, he can immediately repeat that video to try to satisfy his desire for resolution. He can also send that video to friends and embed the video on his own site, thereby exponentially increasing distribution virally very quickly. As a result, songs can achieve mass audiences of millions within a few days, increasing royalties rapidly. Given the popularity of the site, it is only a matter of time before it also affects chart positioning.

So in the new paradigm, the next "Wannabe" will be poised to be highly effective from day one. The user can keep playing the song on demand over and over to his heart's content. Each time, royalties will rack up, and the artist will climb the charts more rapidly. And listeners will not have to wait weeks for radio programmers to determine if the audience wants the song repeated regularly. These songs will now storm up the charts in a matter of days. Ironically, it will be a double-edged sword for record labels. They will be happy when they have such a hit, and disappointed when another track that comes out of left field usurps the record they had planned to slowly climb the charts.

The smarter musicians, however, can plan for this by integrating the technique into their stronger songs. Instinct would suggest this could only happen with shorter songs, which runs counter to the argument in Chapter Two that longer songs are necessary. The answer is that if done well, this technique can create so many multiple listening situations that a short three-minute song, in effect, becomes a six-minute song. The extra-added benefit is that it can then be counted toward two plays on an airplay chart. It is also very possible for long songs to employ this technique. With their length, they likely would not get as many multiple plays as shorter songs, but every multiple play is a good one.

Do not forget that each successive multiple play also prevents another song from being heard. A person's listening session is finite, so songs that can manipulate themselves into repeat listens cancel out someone else's song, which will go unheard. Technology is making it that much easier for anyone to put a song out, but anyone wishing to make a living off of music needs to employ as many tricks as possible to generate a living wage from royalties. Keeping other songs from being played while simultaneously making your song more desirable is easily a double win. The chart bump this type of song receives, coupled with the chart depression it delivers to other songs, becomes a fringe bonus in the quest to get the song noticed.

NENA

The Spice Girls employed this technique only once. After that, their hits featured more conventional endings. German pop star Nena, with her sole 1980s hit, "99 Luftballons," had only that moment of success worldwide, but she utilized a similar technique to engage multiple listens. Her song repeated the intro at the end.

This is another example in which the listener can feel incomplete. The natural expectation of the listener in "99 Luftballons" is that he will hear the meaty, bouncy chorus one more time before the song ends. Instead, the song leaves the listener hanging on for an ending that never comes. Employing a false ending by restructuring the song to deliberately leave out a final chorus can be equally effective.

With the ability of repeat listenership so readily available, songs that start with the chorus can also work to maximum benefit. As suggested earlier, placing the chorus in the first seven seconds of the song will help suck listeners in. If the chorus is omitted from the song's ending, the listener's immediate desire is to hear that chorus again so the song can be resolved in his head. If that chorus is at the beginning of the song (and not just at sixty seconds in), the user can access his favorite portion of the song immediately, instead of needing to fast forward to the proper spot. Instinctively, most users will remember this, and act on satiating that desire. This, in turn, will produce a higher likelihood of that repeat listen.

Nena never went on to produce another U.S. hit, despite all the elements that earned her a hit single. The pop landscape is littered with artists like her who shine for one brief moment. Then, due to any number of reasons, they never repeat their success and become just a footnote in music history. With listening habits changing the elements of a hit song, one-hit wonders will likely occur more often, not less.

6

CREATE MORE
ONE-HIT WONDERS

The masses have always been more interested in an individual song than a whole album. At its purest form, an album is just a group of songs put together. In many instances, these songs contain a common thematic element, which is what gives an album's songs consistency. In more cases, this common thematic element is little more than just utilizing the same technicians for an entire album: Producer, engineer, mixer, songwriters, etc.

SPORTS AND MUSIC

In that regard, an album and the economics thereof are much more akin to a sports team and its scales of economics. Take a classic album such as Nirvana's *Nevermind*. The legacy that this album has created can easily be compared to a classic sports team such as the New England Patriots in 2003. The album's equivalent to this team is not any one game the Patriots played, but, in fact, the entire season. People reminisce about how Tom Brady led a team that finally jelled into what people called a "dynasty." The team worked through an entire season building on fundamentals and becoming the Super Bowl Champions for the second time in three years. That was also the start of an NFL record twenty-one consecutive wins over that season and the one that followed. Throughout, they had virtually the same players and coaches, and the back-end office support to make sure they were also a successful business.

Sports fans think of the season as an entirety. They also remember the elements of specific games that made it such a memorable season, most notably the winning score drive in the Super Bowl with only a minute left to play. These are the elements that play over and over in SportsCenter highlight reels, and make up the legacy that the team created. These are, in essence, the songs that make up the "album" of the entire season.

This analogy provides added support for the album as a continued format that must be saved. The Super Bowl and the LPs came into vogue during the same era about half a century ago. This is plenty of time for people to feel that both are institutions that have always been around. But they could also fade away as relics of a bygone time.

Legacy can certainly drive the economics of a business. When this is done successfully, a particular legacy can be the driving economic factor of the entire business. The Super Bowl has certainly become a master of obtaining massive broadcast revenues and corporate sponsorships. But these large revenues are little more than big profits for few people in the business as a whole.

When you get into the micro dynamics of the sports industry, you see that the dollars do not come from one big final game. They also rarely come from that entire team dynasty. Revenues actually come in game by game. When people want to see a game live, they have the option of purchasing season tickets that give them access to every single game, or purchasing single tickets to the games of their choice.

The majority of game attendees are not season ticket holders. This can be due to a lack of funds, but for most people, there is not enough time or desire to experience

every single game. Some games are going to be big defeats.
Some games are going to occur at inconvenient times in that
person's life.   Some games are worth paying for, while
others are only worth seeing free on TV.

Yet some people also come to the game and buy shirts,
food, and countless other accoutrements. Other people also
come to the game and never drop a dime on merchandise or
concessions. Still other people never show up to a single
game, but do buy the shirt, etc. These are not just multiple
revenue streams—they acknowledge the variety of ways that
people integrate sports into their lives.

The record industry has spent most of the last thirty years
insisting that everyone should be a season ticket holder, and
very few should only attend the occasional game. This is
part of the drama that has resulted in the financial woes the
music industry has been suffering. Much like sports, the
music industry makes it very difficult for an artist to have a
winning game every time out. The buying public will accept
a losing game every once in awhile, but if you lose too
many, season ticket sales go down, and the only individual
games that will sell well are the "good" games. Conversely,
season ticket sales will start increasing if the team has a
consistent winning streak and championship season.

There is every reason that the music business, which like
sports is another form of entertainment, should look at its
fans and buyers in the same fashion. Concentrate on making
a consistent winning streak (i.e. hit songs) so people will be
compelled to purchase the entire season (i.e. an album). It
actually has been the adage that labels have been working on
achieving. The model is flawed because it is built on
economics that it can *only* survive on the season ticket
holder.

For every winning Super Bowl team, there are also thirty-
one teams that do not win. Of those, an additional eleven
make it to at least the first level of the playoffs, while the
remaining twenty sit home on the couch. It is those twenty
teams that survive with merchandise sales, TV licensing, and

single ticket sales. They have to make hits off of non-hit seasons, sometimes via compelling matches or marketing incentives such as cheaper tickets or ball days.

Occasionally, though, these teams break through and have a brief winning season. The NFL showed that several times in 2005. The Seattle Seahawks made it to the Super Bowl for the first time in history. The Indianapolis Colts started the season at 13-0, only the fourth team in league history to do so. These teams went on to sustain several years of glory. Sports history suggests that when the lineups of the teams age and/or change, the success may be difficult to maintain.

MOVING AWAY FROM ONLY SEASON TICKET HOLDERS

The music industry's proposed move from a model of only season ticket holders to both season and individual ticket holders is going to be a rocky one. For one thing, it takes a long time to convince someone to back a team for an entire season. It also takes several years within this paradigm for a consistent type of team (or artist) to prove worthy of a deeper financial consumer commitment.

In the process, income needs to be generated, and it must do so rapidly for big record companies. Simultaneously, in our analogy, consumers have become excited about being able to experience single games once again. This confluence will likely result in several years of mostly single-game experiences. It will take a significant amount of time before a consumer is willing to commit to an artist for a complete "season."

Consequently, no matter how good or bad an artist is, many artists will not be able to sustain a career past one or two hit songs. The environment itself is not going to be conducive enough for many artists to have a prolonged body of work. As such, the foreseeable future will be looked back at as one that produced many hit songs, but very few hit artists. Even artists of quality will likely find listeners unwilling to give their other works sustained consideration, as consumers will be distracted by a combination of factors that will subconsciously prevent them from exploring an artist's catalog.

In this environment, many one-hit wonders will actually produce plenty of perceived hits, and these will come from a diverse array of musicians. Listeners, too, will experience a variety of different styles, instead of limiting their choices to a single artist. The sheer volume of releases hitting the market bears this out. From 2000 to 2005, the number of album releases doubled from 30,000 a year to 60,000 a year. And this was in a time when overall sales declined precipitously. If someone were to attempt to listen to every song released in its entirety every hour of every day, it would only be physically possible to hear about 5-10% of released material.

The reason why so many new artists and labels would even enter this fray is due to a combination of reduced start up costs along with the newfound freedom users have to experience fewer songs across a broader platform of artists. The quality of other songs by a particular artist is irrelevant to the diversity the listener now experiences.

The novelty of technology's advances is unlikely to change this behavioral pattern for several years. People will simply gravitate to picking and choosing hits and will ignore other unfamiliar songs. With so much variety instantly accessible, the consumer would rather spend time experiencing the best that multiple artists have to offer than experience what the best artist offers up in multiple ways. One can fight this notion because he feels it is unjust, but that is an exercise in futility. Technology dictates consumption. The ability to experience and/or purchase "single games" instead of "season tickets" has been a consumer demand that is now readily accessible.

TRENDS OF ONE-HIT WONDERS

There is actually somewhat of a historical precedent to this, and the lessons learned from this period can help everyone understand what the next few years will be like, and how careers can be shaped today in preparation for what is likely to come.

That period was the first half of the 1980s. At this point, despite great strides and increases in the album format throughout the 1970s, the music industry experienced an approximate 20% decline in sales coming into the decade. Added difficulty arrived in the form of music television, which overnight changed the dynamics and marketing of a hit song. Not only did an artist have to make good music, but he also had to create compelling visuals to go along with it. This also meant the artist had to be visually appealing.

Given all these factors, the era is mostly remembered for artists who had only one hit: Kajagoogoo, Dexy's Midnight Runners, Toni Basil, Michael Sembello. Several of them even made up some of the #1 songs mentioned in Chapter One. And some did have platinum albums, while others had only platinum singles. Sadly, some, while big at radio and in the memory of millions of people, never really made significant money for the performance of the song.

In the music industry, such a song is often referred to as a "Turntable Hit." This means that while the song was enormously successful at radio, it did not produce enough sales to match the dollars spent on obtaining the massive radio airplay. Add in promotional touring expenses, recording costs, publicity, and retail promotion, and you find many situations where the label was lucky to break even.

When a record did sell, even though the public felt only one song on the album was "good," word of mouth often took so long that the album had already sold gold or platinum by the time the masses realized it was not terrific. Without the Internet reaching people worldwide, only little microcosms of local communication existed. Therefore, it would take several hundreds of thousands of little "word of mouth" events to occur before an album developed a negative reputation. By that time, the record label very possibly would have pulled out a profit.

As multi-national corporations bought record labels in the late 1980s and early 1990s, they did several things that had an impact on the one-hit wonder. First, they put more emphasis on the multi-hit album. Rather than spending a lot of money to squeeze the most out of one radio hit, they placed their bets on records that became phenomenons. Through this, artists such as Hootie & the Blowfish, Shania Twain, and Alanis Morissette went on to sell over ten million copies of a single album. When this happened often enough to move from a "once in a decade" feat to a regular occurrence, the Recording Industry Association of America (RIAA) established a new award certification, the "Diamond," to mark this now regular sales threshold.

One-hit wonders did not go away, nor were they likely to do so. In order to maximize profits from these acts and drive full album sales, record labels began deleting singles before they achieved maximum sales, and then not releasing them at all. Until the mid-1990s, singles were an established entry point for young music consumers who could not afford full albums with their meager allowances. But this also allowed people to purchase the artist's only hit when it was viewed as the only good song on the album. This new strategy worked successfully with some acts for a brief period: Hanson scored only one #1 hit, but they managed to sell four million albums from it, along with 1 1/2 million singles.

Since single sales were necessary for positioning on the *Billboard* Hot 100, the number of one-hit wonders that topped the chart dropped precipitously during this period. The labels continued to realize large profits from albums, which fed their need to establish multiple hits or sales from these records. One of the biggest hits of the era, Chumbawamba's "Tubthumping," failed to hit the #1 slot despite its widespread popularity. This was largely due to the label pressing only about 100,000 copies of "Tubthumping," making it impossible to gain value for the effect single sales had on chart positioning.

With a magic formula for profits in effect, the need to gain sustained success for a one-hit wonder diminished rapidly. The big profits were in the multi-hit albums. Adding insult to injury, the press decried one-hit wonders as being a major component for the failings of the music industry. An album with only "one good song" selling for twenty bucks or more was seen as the great consumer rip-off. Music fans spoke with closed wallets.

The reality was that during this period, record labels had already begun to move away from signing one-hit wonders. The big successes of pop bands such as *NSYNC, R&B acts like Destiny's Child, and rock bands like Creed came about because they had great albums with multiple satisfying songs. With few single sales influencing the Top 100 chart, the climate for a one-hit wonder to even make the chart became nearly impossible. With no sales and no chart action, acts with only one solid hit quickly became persona non grata, and rumors of numerous artists never even seeing a release date increased during this period. The fact that these were artists with only one potential hit is very likely a reason for these business decisions.

The end result was a twelve-year stretch from 1993 to 2005 that produced the fewest one-hit wonders in pop music history. In 2006, the tide began to change. With the popularity of iTunes and its growing influence on the chart, more #1 one-hit wonders were released than the previous six years combined. Only time will tell if some of these solo hitmakers since 2006 produce another hit, but industry wisdom is presuming that acts like D4L, Daniel Powter, and Mims will be unable to replicate their chart heights again.

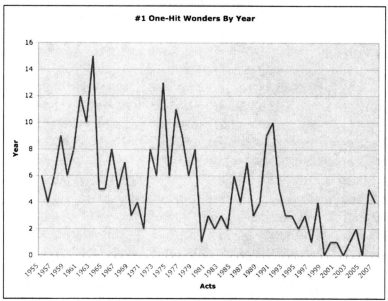

CHART SOURCE: *BILLBOARD/JOEL WHITBURN'S TOP POP SINGLES 1955-2006*

PROFITS FROM ONE HIT

Selling singles digitally proves to be a very economical way to distribute and profit from a sole hit. With little in the way of manufacturing costs that previously made singles a break-even scenario at best, hit digital singles can gross high six figures to make back at least a significant portion of the initial song production and marketing expenses. Now that one-hit wonders are becoming a business necessity, many labels are signing acts explicitly for that purpose, and by budgeting accordingly, are profiting quite nicely.

A hit song now also brings ringtone and ringback sales. These incomes, initially viewed as ancillary, are now quickly becoming major portions of revenue. These returns can also be in the high six figures, which combined with track sales, can result in over a million dollars in sales for a single hit.

The one-hit wonder can now also generate streaming royalties. When radio played these "turntable hits," the

record company failed to see any performance royalties, despite the song's popularity on the airwaves. Now, this same popularity on online and satellite radio services can easily result in dollars that contribute to a song's overall financial success. These were initially in the high five figures, but have quickly grown to six figures for many hits.

The music video, once seen as a necessary marketing loss, now generates income. The interesting change is that the music video no longer needs television to generate success. Instead, it finds success online, where legitimate services pay royalties to the major labels. These royalties do not always cover the production costs, but they do help recoup a substantial portion of these expenses and can also generate five or six figures in income.

As a result, production costs for most music videos have dropped. By keeping costs down and driving up traffic to the video online, videos are becoming a profitable item in their own right. User-generated videos are also created at no cost to the artist or label, but the music usage can, in fact, generate dollars, as every usage counts as a royalty payment to that artist. A novelty hit such as Right Said Fred's "I'm Too Sexy" may have previously been unable to sell albums, but the song is now likely generating significant royalties, as many people utilize the song as a reference point in the homemade videos they share with the world. Rick Astley's "Never Gonna Give You Up" may have been the subject of an Internet prank called "Rick-Rolling" in 2008, but the subsequent streaming play and digital track sales easily resulted in six figures of quick passive income.

If the performer is viewed from the start as being more about a "song" rather than artistry, labels are less concerned about lifetime imaging. With that, a label will aggressively look for all possible licensing opportunities, as these will not affect the long-term imaging for the artist. If the song is catchy enough to, indeed, generate that one hit, the label should have no difficulty in securing commercial, TV, and movie placements to the tune of low six figures.

So, when all revenue streams are put together, a solid one-hit wonder can likely gross between two and four million dollars. This is certainly a decent income stream that most companies would love to have. What makes this revenue more enticing is that it comes with lower expenditures than in previous years. By keeping costs low and income high, these scenarios will quickly become the bread and butter of many label rosters.

THE CONSCIOUS ONE-HIT WONDER

Strategizing around one hit carries over into the recording process. Production for an album usually requires enough time in the studio to complete at least ten songs. Despite the fact that one song usually carries the sales of the other nine, the dollars spent on producing each song are often relatively equal. (That is presuming the artist uses a production team of equal caliber on all the songs, if not the same production team.) If an artist comes in with the knowledge that he has only one potential hit, the label can save money by not even recording other songs. Everyone can focus on making just the one hit and perhaps a couple of other songs, and spend production money only on those.

When the record is ready to ship to radio, the label no longer has to spend the quarter to half-a-million dollars previously required to break a song. With the recent anti-payola investigations fully settled, record companies no longer need to pay steep incentives to force radio airplay. While money is still spent in other ways to secure airplay, the overall expense has been greatly reduced.

The cost of positioning the record at retail is also greatly reduced. The physical outlets do not have the mechanics to sell digital singles, and a one-hit wonder has little chance to sell full-length records. Therefore, the expense of paying for prime placement in the stores is no longer needed.

Additionally, manufacturing and shipping costs are also reduced, if not outright eliminated.

This is not to say that marketing a one-hit wonder will come cheaply. A label will still need the dollars to make a video, find the right stylist, and hire teams to do promotions and marketing. However, these all occurred within the physical world. Costs are greatly reduced in the new hit-making environment, where previously, many millions of dollars might have been spent in artist development prior to anything hitting the marketplace.

The added benefit with these lower expenditures is that the opportunity exists for a one-hit wonder to become a hit artist. The above route provides record labels a low-cost marketplace entry to test the public's reaction to a certain sound, style, or image for a particular artist. If it, indeed, takes hold and the public clamors for more, the label is able to spend relatively modest funds to find the next hit artist.

When that artist is discovered, he will also be set on an entirely new path to song distribution. Success and profitability will occur without the normal industry mechanics. In fact, the artists themselves will have found a new way to satisfy their audience, become more profitable, and indulge their creative musings at the same time. And the way to do it is certainly not by holding back eleven songs until the twelfth one is ready.

7

RELEASE MORE SONGS
MORE OFTEN

The Supremes had thirty-two Top Forty hits in eight years. The Beatles had forty-six Top Forty hits in seven years. In the heady days of the singles-based record business, the industry was set up to produce that volume of hits. Recording was basic. Radio was hungry to constantly get and play the next huge record from the big artists. What happened in the forty years between that era and now?

Destiny's Child, essentially this generation's Supremes, had thirteen Top Forty hits in eight years. Matchbox Twenty, about the biggest pop/rock hit-making machine of the last decade, has made ten Top Forty hits in seven years. In these profitable days of the album-based record business, the industry squeezed more money out of fewer hits. Ironically, the ability to record more affordably grew in recent years. Radio, though, got more expensive, and was more content to be a slave to call-out research. With consolidation and companies going public, radio had to grow revenues to ever-larger heights. If a station had to take a risk, they needed to get something in return to justify it. Once the risk paid off, they had to milk it for all it was worth. This meant record companies, when trying to get airplay for an artist's second single, were constantly told, "The first single isn't finished."

FEWER HITS MEANS FEWER PROFITS

The net result is that in the effort to maximize profits out of every release, hit artists are producing fewer songs. Fewer songs means fewer profitable copyrights for all parties, which in the long run means fewer dollars, no matter how much money was squeezed out of that initial window. The Beatles doubtfully thought they would make millions of dollars forty years after the fact via a group of French circus clowns. Yet, in 2006, when Cirque de Soleil produced the spectacle *Love*, which mashed up dozens of timeless Beatles classics, that is exactly what happened. Had the Beatles not actually recorded a few hundred songs and made a high percentage of them hit worthy, there would be no catalog to make the show, even if the desire were there.

This is not even limited to the biggest stars of that bygone era. Frankie Valli and the Four Seasons were also respectable hit makers at that time, notching up twenty-eight Top Forty hits in the 1960s and then three more with a mini-comeback in the 1970s. But in 2005, they managed to have enough hits to justify a Broadway musical about them (*Jersey Boys*), which was almost entirely comprised of their songs. In the past few decades, only the most prolific top hit makers could hope for a similar large-scale production in their future.

This should not be the case in the modern music business. Amazingly, artists chart fewer hits despite the fact that it is infinitely easier to record, experiment, and create that music. Computer technology has now put the power of high-quality recording studios in the homes of nearly everyone who wants it. No need to have a full band playing each note precisely in one take anymore. ProTools multi-tracking technology allows one person to create every instrument himself without wondering if the bass player will show up.

But even if the artist creates more music, record labels appear to be more risk-averse. There are increasing rumors of rejected songs and albums from artists that were not deemed "hit worthy." This restraint may have yielded short-term gains. While the industry standard of hit making has been widely presumed to be around 10%, that figure has crept up substantially in recent years. A gold record or better is the rule of thumb for a successful album run, but nearly 20% of the new major label releases hit that benchmark each year. If you take out low-selling, but still profitable releases such as live albums or niche genre music, the actual number of profitable hits is likely to be higher. The label to which an artist is signed also has a lot to do with it. Half of the labels had a hit percentage below 20%, but half of them scored higher than that.

The key lies in that bottom 80% of sales. An obvious failure occurs when a label spends millions of dollars to launch a particular artist, only to get thousands back in return. But what if a label spent tens of thousands and made hundreds of thousands? What if this happened cumulatively and more often? A label would certainly stand to make more money, not less.

MAKING COPYRIGHTS

Most labels forget that they should be in the business of one thing: Making copyrights. When big record companies purchase independent labels, they do not always acquire them to capitalize on their hipper talent roster. Instead, they look to expand the catalog of exploitable copyrights. If that catalog is bigger and mightier than the catalog of the guy across the street, then they look brighter and bolder than their competitors.

But buying copyrights of new brand names is not as safe a business model as building extensions of name brands that already exist. For years, the soft drink business built up multiple brands to exploit. Coca-Cola, for example, developed Sprite for its clear lemony drink, and Tab for its diet cola. Many of those brand extensions worked, but in the 1990s, the company realized that the more successful approach was to just call these new flavors Coke, no matter how far they strayed from the family tree. Do you remember OK Cola? Not trading on the brand name is now largely a liability. So what normally might have been a new name for Black Cherry soda is now Black Cherry Vanilla Coke. It is cheaper to extend and play off the existing brand.

So why do major labels insist on limiting the brand extensions of their artists by not creating as many copyrights? Coke knows that Black Cherry Vanilla Coke will not sell as much as regular Coke. Therefore, it does not spend as much money to market it. Labels can take the same approach. If an artist releases a song that is undeniably *not* a hit, then the label should not try to market it as one. The record company should aim it directly and succinctly to the faithful, but not try to penetrate the dense pop world. That way, the song has presence, and the artist does not get upset that his hard work has gone unheard. It is not left on a virtual shelf, and may even surprise everyone and become a hit naturally.

Most importantly, it will generate dollars. If you are working on cultivating the artist as a brand, the brand pipeline must be continually filled. Why does Coke spend hundreds of millions of dollars on their main brand *and* their brand extensions every year? Surely the world knows about Coke. No live music fan ever goes into a club and orders a "Jack and Pepsi." But Coca-Cola knows if it stops marketing for even a minute, the competition will swoop down and take away its consumers. And every consumer who goes away runs the risk of potentially never coming back.

Yet time and time again, record labels willingly let their artists' fans go away for extended periods of time. Every time the artist has a significant lull between releases, he loses his fan base. If you are the Beatles and are just *that* good, that is fine. But most artists are not in that league. And there is likely another artist out there who can fill the same need in a person's life should a particular artist go away temporarily.

THE SPEED OF SONG

Add to that factor the youthfulness of most artists' audience. If an artist takes three years between records, it may not seem like a long time. But consider this: A kid could discover the artist toward the end of his freshmen year of high school, and that record could be the soundtrack for his first official high school summer. The artist should be cemented with that kid, correct? If you wait three years, the next record would likely come out in his *senior* year of high school. To teenagers, the difference between freshman and senior year is nearly a lifetime. Most seniors look back on things in their freshman year as "kids' stuff." In that environment, do you want to be the artist who has to convince that teenager all over again that you are just as good? In essence, the artist has to start over in building that teenager's loyalty.

Compounding the industry's woes is a distribution system that is rapidly becoming antiquated in a digital society. This problem is exacerbated by today's promotional system, which disseminates music faster than ever. Just a decade ago, if a song by a hot artist got "leaked" to an influential radio station, it would still take a few days, production rush charges, and some expensive FedEx bills to get that song out to all the appropriate radio stations in the country. Now, if one radio station gets that leak, every station in the country can have the track emailed to them in a matter of minutes, so almost everyone can play it at the same time. This process is improved by the computerization of radio stations (very few actually play the music off of CDs, vinyl, or "cart" tapes anymore), along with the consolidation of radio ownership. One radio station programmer can instantly e-mail every programmer in his company, giving them a slight competitive advantage in all cities.

With promotional distribution no longer an issue, there is still no guarantee that a person listening to the radio station would actually hear the song. Even though many stations play these hits ad nauseum (as often as once an hour in some cases), radio listenership has been declining, and the Internet is claiming large numbers of those listeners. With Internet distribution, songs can ascend both charts and public consciousness in an increasingly rapid fashion.

It also means these songs will "burn out" more quickly than they had in the past. While there are enormous amounts of entertainment options for music listeners, these same consumers are finding and consuming songs more rapidly. Presuming that most songs are good, but not exceptional, there is little to keep them glued to the listener's consciousness for a significantly long period of time. Unfettered access also allows them to experience--and in some cases over-consume--these songs in virtually no time at all.

Meanwhile, the methods by which the bulk of a song's income is generated remains stuck in an ancient system that is slow to respond to rapid shifts in trends. If a new pop singer hits the airwaves, a record label typically gives that artist three to five months to lay roots in the marketplace before the CD is released into stores. Even if a label wanted to change this, it would have great difficulty. The major retail outlets (Wal-Mart, Target, Best Buy) require a one to two-month period before the record's release to ascertain potential sales, obtain the marketing buy from the label, place the order, send the order to a distribution center, distribute to the stores, and then stock the shelves. Even then, they may not order the disc unless they know there is awareness that will generate sales.

Then, even if retail could circumvent much of the back-office procedures, manufacturing and shipping realities mean that a CD would need at least two weeks to physically appear in these outlets. In 2008, the Raconteurs became the first major artist to test the waters on changing this model. They announced that shortly after completing their record, they would release the album to everyone in one week's time. This rapid release appeared to sell as many copies in its first week as it would have with a significant marketing set-up. This will likely be regarded as an effective test that may slowly move the entire industry in this direction in the coming years.

While all this occurs, artist and label personnel are operating in a world where things move more rapidly, which then means that their work efforts also move at a faster clip. This is also a community of people who are generally insular, over-worked, and afraid that they will fail in a business where large sales have become difficult to achieve. As a result, many work themselves into a knot, over-thinking nearly every situation that then negatively impacts each project.

SPEED VS. PERFECTION

When people first begin dating while teenagers, they often develop an ideal persona of a perfect mate. Over time, a person changes this profile and backs away from their original vision as the realization that an absolutely perfect companion is nearly impossible to find. With divorce rates hovering around 50%, people become skittish about choosing a life partner. The net result is the average age that a person marries has increased about one year a decade. At the end of the twentieth century, it stood at about 24 1/2 for women and about 26 for men, the highest average age for marriage ever recorded for either sex. The more time people have, the more they second-guess their decisions. This delays the process at best, and at worst, prevents a decision from even being made.

Striving for perfection, while certainly an ideal to work toward, is a significant hurdle in the creation of music, too. Much of the music of past decades, even that beloved by millions of people, is filled with mistakes. The reason is that it was often too costly and time-consuming to fix it. Some mistakes were acceptable, as the song was therefore "good enough." When there are ample amounts of time between completion of song production and marketplace release, it results in equally ample amounts of worry about wrong decisions that may have been made. During this period, executives, artists and consultants alike will tinker and recreate, adding additional expenses, and delaying the generation of income for the project. These are situations that can no longer be afforded.

What happens is that a new pop singer will have a song released that is hot at that moment. Hoping to drive first week sales of the full album, some record labels refrain from offering the single for sale by digital music stores, believing they will have much greater sales of the album once it does arrive in stores. In many cases, the opposite actually occurs. When a song is hot, the demand for owning that song is immediate. The Internet age has created a consumer expectation that nearly all entertainment should be available at one's fingertips at the exact moment of discovery. In many cases, music fans will gladly accept an affordable, legal way to receive this music. What they will not accept is not being able to get that song at that particular moment. If they cannot, they will use illegal means to get the song instantly.

Today, the notion of holding back music to create a big sales splash has everything to do with egos and very little to do with savvy business sense. Sales need to occur at the moment of impact, when the song is hot to the core consumer. If they do not, they evaporate with increased piracy. However, even if labels traded in some chart positioning for sales, the antiquated system of manufacturing and retail would prevent the adequate stocking and positioning of hit records in an extremely rapid fashion.

SHIFTING AN ALBUM-BASED ECONOMY

This presents a significant problem for the industry as a whole. The album-based economy is predicated on collecting multiple songs and holding them back for a simultaneous release on one date in physical form. With the world moving at a more rapid pace than a physical based system can possibly allow, how can a label be profitable in this environment? How can a label continue to even make stars as the mechanics in the star-making machinery have changed so rapidly?

The album mold, therefore, no longer becomes the most profitable method of financial success for most artists. If anything, it has actually become the Achilles heel for the music industry. The reliance on an album-based economy leads to increased production expenditures, inability to properly react to marketplace demands, costly delays due to various production cycles—and as consumers have often spoken about—an overall decrease in the actual quality of the music.

Changing to an economy whereby the artist and songwriter release more songs is necessary for survival, even though the true financial solvency of such a move might not be evident for several years. Its trajectory into the marketplace, however, is a necessary occurrence, and only with proper foresight and planning can it become a financially lucrative one.

The digital delivery system is set up so that any number of songs can be released at a given time. This can create a scenario whereby an artist releases the number of songs that are deemed fruitful, based on the output achieved via recording sessions. An artist can book one week with a producer and studio, and if the net results are two tracks, he can release two tracks. If there are five tracks, he can release five. The important thing is that the songs get released, and released swiftly.

Part of the reason many timeless songs are a part of one's psyche is because someone marketed them as a single. This gave the song an aura and spotlight that other songs by that artist did not have. Whether the song became hit worthy is somewhat irrelevant. Over time, many #1 songs are only remembered slightly, while others that barely cracked the charts are considered classics. The common thread, however, is that in nearly all cases, a record company chose to focus its energies around that one song for a period of time, thereby elevating that song above the others.

MARIAH CAREY VS. RICKY MARTIN

In the album-based format, the amount of singles released to the marketplace often depends on the success of the full-length product. Mariah Carey's *The Emancipation of Mimi* sold ten million copies worldwide, and subsequently her label, Island Def Jam, released seven songs as singles, with four becoming big hits. This occurred despite her spotty track record in the years preceding the album release. Meanwhile, around the same time, Ricky Martin's album, *Life,* came out with a massively hyped single, "I Don't Care," featuring rap stars Fat Joe and Amerie. The song never gained traction and the album sold poorly. The only follow-up single, "Drop It On Me," gained so little traction that it was quickly abandoned.

There are two primary reasons for this. The first is that record labels, like most businesses, must engage in risk management. If what they consider to be the artist's best song barely makes an impact, they presume that the songs usually deemed less worthy will almost certainly have no success in the marketplace. Therefore, they believe, it is not worth the marketing expenditures to promote those songs as singles. The second reason is that the music industry at large is quick to assign failure to artists and projects that do not gain quick traction with the public. Image often becomes reality, and many old-guard gatekeepers view one dud by one artist as a sign that the artist will never achieve success.

All of those forays into risk management, however, are sometimes poor assessments of the real situation. Risk management is also about setting expectations. In the 1950s and 1960s, singles climbed up the charts, peaked, and then fell off in favor of the next single. The first three singles by the Supremes were all duds. The fourth, "When the Lovelight Starts Shining Through His Eyes," was only a modest success. It took until single number six before they found the magic formula that led to so many hits—a nearly two-year process. Motown, their record label likely managed and manipulated that process so that both industry and fans could feel that they were getting aboard a rising tide. In the 1970s and 1980s, that process shifted toward albums. Bruce Springsteen signed his record deal in 1972. Yet it took until 1986 before Bruce Springsteen had the first box set of albums ever to debut at #1 on the charts with *Live/1975-85.*

All of this happened with a great degree of impropriety that was an inherent flaw in the system. The chart companies had to trust that the people responsible for reporting information (radio, record stores, jukebox companies) were being honest. The truth was far from that. Stories abounded of electronics, drugs, and hard cash exchanging hands for the secure manipulation of the chart. That Bruce Springsteen #1 debut? When the label was rumored to accept a large quantity of returns, one could surmise that the record-making debut had more to do with the numbers retailers *said* they sold, rather the amount of units that actually moved across the cash register.

The expectations of the gatekeepers through the 1980s were simply to develop an artist and work with him over time to grow into a success. As long as there were measurable results along the way, one could count on the industry and fans being a part of that success. Sometimes those expectations were set out over weeks, and in the case of some rock acts, over years. But nobody expected or wanted an artist to be a sensation overnight. Even those perceived overnight sensations, such as the *Saturday Night Fever* soundtrack, occurred with a phenomenon that had been well documented in big cities for several years. It was also carried by a pop act (Bee Gees) that had developed a solid reputation over the previous decade. This was not an out-of-nowhere success.

Entering the 1990s, the record labels had to change their manipulation game with the advent of two new tracking innovations. Broadcast Data Systems (BDS) electronically monitored radio signals so programmers could no longer lie about how many times they played a song. SoundScan monitored barcode transactions so retailers could no longer fudge how many copies of an album they sold. The net result was finding out that the hits sold more quickly than anyone previously realized. Radio was also much more likely to play that hit song right when it was hot, because that was what the audience demanded. None of it was new. This was just the first time it all became so concrete.

These electronic measuring systems showed that something was perceived to be a hit when it happened quickly. Record company personnel often complain that an act gets four weeks to prove something in the marketplace before the "suits" cut their losses. Gatekeepers are so used to seeing these spikes, and dealing with a high volume of releases, that they can only effectively respond to those songs that strike fast and hard. Similarly, if the album does not sell at the top of the charts, the perception is that the album will not happen and the industry moves on to the next project. The bottom line is that the project either hits or it does not, and those quick-minded decisions that Malcolm

Gladwell outlines in his book, *Blink*, becomes the majority of the moves made by the industry.

So what are the changes in expectation setting and risk management, and how do they relate to the volume of songs being released? Part of the answer lies in the relationship between the artist and the song. They are fundamentally partners, but not the same unit. In the Ricky Martin example above, the expectation was that one song failed, so an entire project failed. The only thing that truly failed was the song. Record executives can hope, but not reasonably expect, that every song by their A-level artists will be a hit. If a particular style, sound, or song subject does not work, the A&R department and artist management can adjust the strategies with new songs.

The issue with Ricky Martin's album is that the record label recorded at least ten songs around a particular image and idea before they truly knew if that was the proper sales direction for the artist. This led to additional production costs that could have been avoided. If the album was recorded all at once in one studio session with the same producer, then an argument could be made that costs were kept to a reasonable level. Today's pop stars rarely do that. In fact, most of them use multiple producers in multiple studios at multiple times throughout the year. The *Life* album contained ten credited producers and essentially five different production set-ups. The lack of musical cohesion around this production and not releasing songs until there were enough for a full-length CD, was actually poor risk management. It increased the financial vulnerability of the entire project.

Consider an alternative strategy for Ricky Martin: The artist records the same single along with one or two others at a session. The song is released with high hopes, but fails to become a hit. The A&R department and management team can then regroup to determine other strategies. They might also receive feedback from industry and fans as to why the single got such a poor reaction. The initial cost savings are evident, but the potential benefit of increased sales from future songs more in line with public expectations can lead to more income.

SHAKIRA

In 2006, another Pop/Latino crossover artist employed almost the exact reverse strategy. It started in early 2005, when Shakira released a Spanish-language album that appealed to her core fan base. The hit single, "La Tortura," hit the mark so perfectly that it became the largest Spanish-language hit ever on English-language outlets, including radio, MTV, and several online outlets.

Later that year, her record company released a companion English language record. The direction, though, moved her away from Latin rhythms and concentrated on a mainstream pop/rock sound. As is industry custom, she recorded eleven like-minded songs for a full-length album. Despite high interest in Shakira from the success of "La Tortura," the resulting single, "Don't Bother," failed to connect with audiences. The resulting initial album sales were softer than anticipated. Shakira sold 400,000 units in the first five weeks of the crucial Christmas season.

In early 2006, the executive team at her record label changed, and the company needed to get its top artist's career back on track fast. A meeting of the minds resulted in some quick creativity in the studio, with Shakira collaborating with producer/rapper Wyclef Jean on the song "Hips Don't Lie." Happily, the song connected in ways that "Don't Bother" never did. It became the biggest song of Shakira's career, and her first #1 single in the United States. It was also the most-played song at radio for 2006 and broke several records in its wake.

But consider the alternative approach of the multiple single. With that scenario, her record label would have recorded a couple of songs in the style of "Don't Bother," and likely found that it was not a wise direction. It would have saved a significant amount of production dollars by *not* recording a full album of material in that style, and the perception of an album that "missed" would not exist in the marketplace. The label would still have regrouped and recorded "Hips Don't Lie," resulting in the same success, but it would have done so under much less duress. As new revenue streams would be a part of that strategy, dollars would still be coming in throughout the process.

When "Hips Don't Lie" was made available for sale, it was added as an additional song on the already existing album that contained "Don't Bother." In an effort to increase sales of the physical CD, the song was not made available for sale digitally. While the resulting sales were strong, there were still many people in the marketplace who had bought the first version of the record, and would not buy the album again just for one song. Without a legal alternative to purchase, these people likely would have stolen the song. Other people who might have bought the record also may have had second thoughts. The perception was that this was not a good record, despite the hit single. As a result, the consumer outlook had it that you would be buying the album only for one song. This likely hampered potential sales.

If the alternative scenario had played out, the record would have had much different momentum. People would have been more apt to purchase the record right out of the gate, as it had a strong single. The perception would not have been one of weakness, since there would not have been a long period of chatter declaring the record as such. Too, there would have been an opportunity to record songs more in line with consumer expectations. And digital revenues would have been coming in, bringing significant income. Ultimately, the record would have likely sold more copies.

But just as important would have been the cost savings on top of the additional income. Studio costs would have been saved by not spending money on more songs that would not work for Shakira's fans. Marketing expenditures on "Don't

Bother" would also have decreased. Since its success would not have been crucial to generate big album sales, the label could have cut marketing costs before they were incurred. This would have exercised proper risk management and minimized losses associated with the song. Because the Shakira album needed a re-release, the label had to spend retail-marketing dollars twice, which could also have been avoided. Finally, the label would likely have realized significant digital sales from not being concerned about cannibalizing album sales.

With the traditional marketing plan, the label's expectations for Shakira were unnecessarily high for a track that, in hindsight, was riskier than initially anticipated. A targeted digital release strategy could have changed expectation levels to a degree that would have generated more income from that momentum. The financial risks would also have been more easily managed by this more strategic output. Instead, the catch-up strategy resulted in spending more marketing dollars that unnecessarily ate into profits.

Another key part of this new risk management is the length of time between albums. Shakira's previous record, the 2001 release *Laundry Service*, was her mainstream breakthrough, and made her a worldwide star across genres. The hits from the record kept coming throughout the year that followed. But after that, she saw the release of only one album, a live record called *Live & Off The Record*, and it did little to keep her name in the public eye. Instead, it was three more years before "La Tortura" brought her back with new music in 2005.

In past decades, three years between releases was unthinkable. Most acts do not have the talent and longevity of Shakira. Waiting that long means running the risk of being forgotten. It also means that artists are not creating during their peak years. Stevie Wonder released four albums in a 2 1/2 year period from 1972 to 1974. These albums are considered some of his masterworks, and are highly revered.

During this same period, he was in a car accident that left him in a coma for four days. Yet he still maintained a higher level of creative output than most artists in recent years.

Stevie Wonder was not alone: Elton John, Led Zeppelin, and the Grateful Dead are among the acts that had similar creative periods. Even pop acts were able to release an album a year during the peaks of their popularity. Acts from the 1980s such as Duran Duran and Culture Club are well remembered for having a lot of hits. But what is often forgotten is that their creative spurts were equally short: They each released three full albums in three years, with a concentrated two-year period of large success in America.

Three years is a long period in the lives of fans under twenty-five, and a lot occurs in those years to shift tastes and desires. As previously mentioned, it is an unrealistic expectation to think that a young freshman Shakira fan will still be a fan by senior year. What about a college sophomore who enters the workforce when the next record is released? How many people consider the artists they listened to in college as being current? And if Shakira has these issues by waiting three years between records, what can we expect for the acts in the tiers below her?

Add to this cocktail the increasingly shorter attention spans of youth, the myriad of musical choices released monthly, and the wealth of older music fans can now easily access. *Then* consider all the other entertainment choices that a person has at his fingertips. Fans feel little loyalty to a particular artist unless that artist consistently feeds that fandom and never leaves its side. To wait three years could result in starting over, with all the budget expenditures that come with breaking a new artist.

Of course, if an artist consistently produces the quality and/or creativity that his audience demands, then taking long periods of time to cultivate pristine work is not only wise, but expected. Radiohead produces a dense layer of electronic-laced progressive rock that easily involves months of intricate song arrangement and production work. They earned their relationship with their fan base over time, and it now allows them the creative freedom to make whatever album they choose in their own timeframe. The result of that, 2007's *In Rainbows*, proved to be a marketing and creative success that actually raised their already large worldwide fan base.

TEEN POP

Most artists, however, are not afforded that freedom. It is certainly no surprise to expect that with pop artists. They often represent a particular moment in time, and their shelf life has a much shorter expiration date. Record labels should make extra effort to have them record and release music with a fair amount of regularity. Consider stars like New Kids on the Block, who were considered the biggest pop stars during their reign atop the charts in the late 1980s and early 1990s. While today their fans would likely think back nostalgically and believe that the group released music for nearly a decade, the truth is that they released five records in five years, including a Christmas and remix record. Of those, four were released during their hot streak of just over two years, from September 1988 to December 1990. Four years later, when the next follow-up was released, the record flopped.

In recent years, artists such as Britney Spears and Backstreet Boys have also employed similar strategies. Britney released six records in seven years. Backstreet Boys also released six records in six years. These totals both include greatest hits records, which represented their strong impact in the market, even if the success of subsequent albums proved elusive. As an example, the Britney Spears record *Blackout,* released eight years after her debut and four years after her previous studio album, sold only 850,000 copies--a little more than 70% less than her poorest selling album of original material. The Backstreet Boys record *Never Gone,* released nine years after their debut and five years after the group's previous studio effort, sold only 750,000 copies--about 7/8 less than their previously poorest selling album of original material. Their greatest success may have been, in fact, the ability to maximize the amount of music released in the narrow window of success.

Another important component of releasing more music is the relationship between artist and fan. The artists who generate the most income over a lifetime are the ones who forge a psychological bond with their fans. When a fan engages this way, he often has a tough time giving up his interest, even if his musical tastes change drastically. Partly out of nostalgia and partly out of obligation, the listener will feel he has already invested a lot of time, energy, and money in an artist's career. If he misses out on future actions by that artist (be they live concerts or music sold), he feels as if he is missing out on important developments.

ALANIS MORISSETTE

If the artist does not engage the listener with enough music quickly, however, the impact might not resonate long term. In the 1990s, artists like Alanis Morissette and Hootie & the Blowfish experienced this firsthand. In the case of Morissette, her breakthrough album, *Jagged Little Pill,* featured songs of intense emotional heartbreak that resonated with people of all ages, but especially with teens and college girls. It was this emotion that propelled her album to sell more than thirty million copies worldwide. Her follow-up record, *Supposed Former Infatuation Junkie,* took three years to make. It sold respectably well, but only about 1/5 of what the first album sold. This was a much larger drop than anticipated from such a big star that touched people so deeply. Despite having other platinum albums, Morissette is largely perceived as a one-album phenomenon, rather than a long-term career artist with millions of fans who will never leave her. Her eight records sold twenty million copies in twelve years. Meanwhile, the Backstreet Boys' six records netted thirty million sold in ten years.

At the point Morissette needed to add depth to her song repertoire, she was placed in an industry machine that had her rehashing the six singles from her big hit album. She had written and released *Jagged Little Pill* by the time she was twenty-one. When she released her next record, she was twenty-four. Those years bring major life changes for any normal person, much less a young woman who became a superstar overnight. Her follow-up single "Thank You" was less concerned about the direct emotion in romantic relationships, and amounted to a meandering stream of consciousness where, among other things, she thanked "silence."

While one cannot accurately predict what might have happened, there is a good possibility that Morissette might have reaped larger benefits by recording songs with more raw emotions during that three-year period, i.e. more captured moments of the turmoil of her youth. This would have given her a deeper catalog of the types of songs that made her famous. It would have also created a deeper psychological connection with her fans. Had she quickly released new music, she would have been reminding her fans that she *continually* spoke to them. If she had done this twice, by the time she reached what became her second album, with its creative meandering musings, her audience would have been more emotionally invested. They would have memorized at least twice as many songs instead of just the collection from the debut. They may have seen more than one concert tour, and they might have even bought several cycles of merchandise. The sheer weight of the fans' physical, mental, and monetary investments through this period would have left them connected to Alanis forever. They would have obliged the less structured second album that did not speak directly to them, feeling as if it were their failure to connect. Instead, when Morissette finally took that journey after a long wait, the fans failed to connect and left.

But the machinations of corporations in the 1990s practically forced that career path upon her. A record company needs to show large quarterly profits. An album that sells itself maximizes profit much more easily. It becomes an easy choice when the corporation focuses on generating more income from the releases with the higher profit margin. The radio stations playing Alanis' music had just hit their stride with the value of call-out research, and were beginning to consolidate into public companies. They also valued maximizing their dollar by playing big hits for longer periods. This created more familiarity, which meant listeners stayed for longer spans of time, allowing radio stations to charge more money for advertisements. Everyone wanted to show large, short-term profits, rather than invest in long-term artists who pay off more over time.

Retailers also started getting squeezed by increasing rents, and so it was more important to give big floor displays to albums that were going to move copies more rapidly. New releases were often a bigger risk. Retailers played it safe and made sure these displays were well stocked with sure things. In addition, big retailers were able to employ computer modeling to predict how many records would sell from week to week. Albums like Morissette's could maximize their sales potential in ways they had never done before.

With digital distribution taking the place of radio, retail, and press, these mechanics are changing rapidly. The most significant is the shifting scale of economics, whereby a particular artist does not necessarily gain maximum profit from milking one release. With personalization options and a wider variety of choices to be had, it is very difficult to convince promotional or retail outlets in the value of pushing to the masses. Much like getting someone hooked on the song, these businesses often give users one shot at responding to a particular artist.

PERSONALIZATION

A personalized retail algorithm on Amazon or iTunes might suggest to that user that they would probably like Alanis Morissette's *Jagged Little Pill,* alongside other recommendations tailored for them. If that user does not respond to that particular recommendation, it becomes increasingly unlikely that the user will get that exact same recommendation again. For one, recommendation engines now look at that artist association less favorably. Another reason is that, to continue maximizing profits, the retailer is more likely to recommend something different rather than continue to recommend something that the user has, consciously or not, already rejected.

Whether digital or physical, the main goal of a retailer remains maximizing shelf space. With mass merchants, they need to be sure that piece of music would fly off the shelf to increase the revenue per square foot in the store. Online retailers adopt the same philosophy. The difference for them is that the revenue per square foot is essentially measured per pixel, as viewed on the pages that the user visits. Since the retailer can identify the shopper, maximization is done through successful recommendation predictions. With that knowledge in mind, it is easy for the retailer to assume that if the shopper passed up that music once, he is highly likely to pass it up again.

Similarly, an online retailer knows that if you have purchased an artist's music once, you are likely to purchase that artist's music again. The retailer will then continue to recommend other titles from that artist. Unlike "implicit" recommendations mentioned above, "explicit" recommendations do not go away so easily. If Amazon thinks you might like something, and then you do not respond, the system will move on to the next recommendation. When Amazon knows that you like the music of a particular artist, it will continue to recommend that artist's music in perpetuity until such a time as the user explicitly states he no longer likes that artist.

Online recommendation algorithms also take into account whether that item had been previously recommended to that particular user, to insure that the user is getting fresh results. By definition, a new title has no prior history, and so there is not one user who could have possibly received that title prior to it becoming available. This would automatically give that title priority for being "explicitly" recommended to users. The retailer knows that users have preferences for new releases by their favorite artists, so it has an extra incentive to employ this system.

Smart artists would immediately recognize the advantages that this system can have in development. The artist can continually release new material to his fan base, keeping his name prominently placed in a user's recommendations list on a regular basis. Since material would continually be new and releases would be in close proximity, the fan would be highly likely to respond. Over time, the psychological factors in hooking that listener to that artist with constant new material will result in consistent interactivity with the music. The listener's commerce will also come from the psychological loyalty of acquiring the artists' complete work at their peak moment of interest.

This also has an additional advantage: It shuts out other artists from being ingrained in a listener's mind over the primary artist. Since recommendations are subject to algorithms that will never be completely precise, anyone giving recommendations almost always puts forth more recommendations than is actually needed. Since the user responds only to one or two recommendations at a given time, if any, the more a user's primary artist releases new material, the more likely the new material prevents the user from responding to the competition.

This runs contrary to the album release, which essentially hoards multiple songs for one big drop. While many people use album recommendations, these are often trickier.

Albums, despite their change in configuration, have not changed in their marketing conceit, and are rapidly becoming outdated. They are created with specific titles and cover art designed to entice buyers into choosing them over all others. The digital proliferation has not just made singles more popular, but it has also changed the relevance of the title and art in the overall marketing of an artist.

ALBUM ART AND TITLES

An obvious change has been the shrinking size of album art. Despite extensive efforts by Apple to include album artwork in both iPod players and iTunes, the reality is that the size of album artwork has shrunk from twelve inches squared to less than one inch squared. With a decrease in size of over 90%, the amount of information that can be communicated by the art to engage a purchase is nearly non-existent. Instead of ornate, detailed artwork, one can only hope for a decent close-up photo, as that is the maximum legibility allotted for proper marketing.

The album title itself is also an element marked for extinction. Titles are largely marketing conceits to describe the contents accurately, so consumers know what they are purchasing. For example, Ella Fitzgerald singing songs by Cole Porter leads to an album entitled *Ella Sings the Cole Porter Songbook.* John Coltrane recorded a concert at a New York jazz club for the subsequent album, *Live at the Village Vanguard.* Titles also originate from the big hit song, making it easy for a buyer to see which album contains the song he wants.

Over time, albums took on more obscure titles, often to represent the moods the artist wanted to convey. Yes's *Tales from Topographic Oceans* accurately describes the four twenty-minute opuses within the album (or one long composition broken up by album sides). The band created the sounds around their studies of Eastern religions, and the title helped communicate the album's contents. Over time, this marketing concept devolved into an unnecessary element that often became indulgent. Quite possibly, these unmarketable album titles may have resulted in lower sales, as important messaging was not communicated to bewildered consumers overwhelmed with choices.

Whether a purchase is made digitally or traditionally, an album title must be explicit in its message if the artist wants a guaranteed sale. Most consumers, even rabid fans, will purchase music on impulse, and they do not have time to decipher hidden messages behind cryptic titles. Labels used to get around this by using large stickers to announce the record's hit song. In the online world, however, there is no equivalent, and the album title has to do the selling alone. Is it possible that Shakira missed many album sales--despite the inclusion of her massive hit, "Hips Don't Lie"--because the record was called *Oral Fixation, Vol. 2*? It is logical that a buyer might be unsure whether the song is on volume one or volume two. Then they might look for volume one, as it would seem right that a big hit would be on an "original" album, not the sequel. But then the buyer might find that there *is* no volume one. That was actually the Spanish-language release *Fijacion Oral, Vol. 1*, which would not even be alphabetically consecutive in Shakira's discography. Traditional marketers of any other product would be shocked if they found that buyers were *not* confused.

With digital retail growing and taking up a significant portion of all sales, albums do not exist anymore—releases do. While there are categories to find titles by album or artist, the song category is typically the dominant field in any digital library. On a micro level, when record companies submit information to digital services, it is done on a song level. An album, then, is just a collection of songs that share the same data in the album field. The result is that databases do not care if in a given week, an artist releases one song, or multiple individual songs, or multiple songs tied to an album. No matter the quantity of the songs, each one is a release in its own right.

Shakira has several songs on her *Oral Fixation, Vol. 2* album, among them the hit, "Hips Don't Lie," and the tried-to-be-a-hit, "Don't Bother." If the strategy of releasing songs separately had been implemented, Shakira would have had an "album" for each of those singles, since they would be considered two separate releases. Each "album" would actually be titled by the name of the single. And recommendations would show up twice as often by being in two separate categories, for album and song. Services do not distinguish between whether an album has one song or one hundred—they just see a release as a pre-designated group of songs.

If most albums were made as they had been before (based on common theme, recording location, or producer), there would possibly be a need to keep the album format. But most albums are recorded in various locations with multiple producers and only the loosest of themes. There is no other reason to continue binding these disparate song elements together, other than for traditions that are now outdated.

By releasing songs separately, the artist and the label would have a better psychological grip on the consumer. They would also continually feed new music to their fan base, have more opportunities for more marketing placements, and continually generate income and copyrights. The downside is that the artist needs to create more music, but that is usually something he wants to do anyway.

Now, to reach even more people, the artist and label need to find the styles, moods and tastes that really connect with the consumer. To reach a mass audience, a song can no longer be as bland as plain yogurt, and smoothly blend in with similar songs on radio. The new mass appeal hit actually needs to be more like gumbo or jambalaya, with a lot of varied ingredients that appeal to a wide group of people. Shakira had those ingredients. More artists and hits will have it as well.

8

APPEAL TO MORE

THAN ONE GENRE

If one acknowledges that the music business is moving back to a singles-based world, one also has to acknowledge other facets of the music consumer's profile as well. An obvious one is that money is made from individual songs, and not off of song packages, which is what albums are. The interesting thing often forgotten or overlooked is the diverse musical tastes of the singles buyer.

In the 1950s and early 1960s, the height of the singles era, music consumers listened to and bought everyone from Elvis Presley to Pat Boone, Bob Dylan to Little Richard, and Johnny Cash to Otis Redding. If you were to make a comparison to today, you might say Justin Timberlake to Michael Buble, John Mayer to 50 Cent, and Alan Jackson to Ne-Yo. Ask radio if this consumer exists, and it acts like each artist operates in his own separate world. Talk to retail, and these artists would likely appear in six separate genre sections in the store (and that includes Internet retailers). But talk to the actual consumers. The number of people who listen to more than one of these acts, if not most of them, would surprise everyone except the fans themselves.

If it is not those acts in particular, the point is still valid. Today's music consumers do not pigeonhole themselves in one genre. The radio model of mass appeal formats has become as antiquated as 78 rpm records. An effective gauge is to ask a rock fan what music he likes. Open-minded rock fans used to answer this question with something to the effect of, "I like all music except country." Now, that answer is usually, "I like all music, and there is even some country I think is cool."

The music fan today is truly a diverse one. Country fans listen to rap. Rap fans find rock that appeals to them. Rock fans even find some pop music cool. When rock critics espouse the virtues of Kelly Clarkson, it is not just an acknowledgement of quality. It is also an acknowledgement that music fans are no longer glued to one type of music. Their tastes now revolve around the song itself, and the fashionable statement of the person singing that song. The genre does not matter.

Still, it is difficult for a music fan to move away from a genre-based system. People still identify themselves as "rock" fans, "hip-hop" fans, or "country fans." The other genres that they enjoy represent the spices that they regularly sprinkle into their musical diets. Just because a rock fan also likes some country does not guarantee that any country hit will make it into that rock fan's musical library. The reverse also holds true. As a result, a song that solely exists in any one genre is unlikely to achieve mass awareness and become a big hit.

ROCK FANS WHO LIKE JAZZ

When you look at the choices that the music consumer has, it is no wonder they are willing to try new musical explorations. Finding music in other genres used to be a chore. Take, for example, a rock fan that liked a little jazz. To discover jazz that he might like required a lot of work. He could listen to a jazz radio station, but the rock fan might only like select amounts of jazz. Listening to hours of jazz just to find songs he liked was too much effort. Never mind that he might like contemporary jazz, but the hour he had available to listen to the radio might have been the "classic jazz" hour. He could explore jazz at a jazz club, but that was subject to the bookings and cover charges of the evening. The rock fan could also learn about jazz via magazines. But an investment in an all-jazz magazine would yield too much information, so he would be unlikely to make that purchase for articles with minutiae about a genre in which he had minimal interest. He might have found a nugget about a potential jazz find in a mass appeal music magazine like *Rolling Stone*. But even then, the fan still had the retail hurdle, where he would have to make a blind faith purchase based on the article in order to hear the music. Since a jazz selection is typically not mass appeal, and outlets made it hard to sample niche titles before purchase, that potential fan would have been unlikely to purchase that album. This pattern often kept people within their safety zone of one primary genre.

Compare this with the avenues that this same fan has to access music today. If the user wants to experience jazz via a radio station, he is no longer relegated to the one jazz station in his city. He can now access thousands of jazz stations scattered throughout the Internet. That contemporary jazz outlet? There are multiple stations that feature just that one style of jazz at any time of the day. Going out to a jazz night club? He can surf the net to find that artist's site prior to getting to the club. That way he knows exactly what sound he will be hearing that evening.

If that same fan wants to find something from knowledgeable jazz writers, he can scour their websites for free and gloss over in-depth articles to find information that is pertinent to his quest. And to find out about a particular artist through normal mainstream channels, he can download a track or two on a peer-to-peer (P2P) site. If thievery affects his consciousness, he can invest a buck or two in downloading a couple of tracks to get a taste of what the artist is like. Add endless, accessible charts that cover the genre, and a casual fan out to find jazz he might like is no longer on a fruitless quest. Instead, his search becomes a quick, enjoyable process that leads to a more diverse musical library.

Once these multiple genres fill someone's musical library, they become part of the listening experience and its multiple forms. The listener could hear a variety of genres, because distinctions such as "most recently added," "most played," or "random" do not discriminate based on genre. The listener just looks at what files fit the baseline criteria and plays them. No longer does someone have to go up and change records or discs to move from genre to genre. The chances that someone might hear multiple genres in one listening session have increased exponentially. The more this occurs, the more that musical variety becomes ingrained as a regular listening experience.

The downside is that all these download or play event experiences are not likely to create hits. Yes, the diversity opens up the music to a much wider cross-section of potential consumers. But as the net widens, so do the available choices. Overall, the number of songs the average consumer can listen to in a meaningful fashion does not increase. So if there are hundreds of thousands of jazz songs for rock fans to potentially appreciate, it would be very difficult for any one of those songs to be the primary beneficiary of this new influx of listeners.

SONGS FIRMLY PLANTED IN ONE GENRE

Another unfortunate side effect will be the appearance of blandness in songs that remain deeply committed to one musical genre. Hanging on to traditional styles will lessen the chance that a new casual fan would actually gravitate to that song. The rock fan that likes some country is more apt to like country that tends to have a hint of rock to it. This could be a country based artist who produces his songs with a bit more electric guitar, such as Keith Urban, or it could be a rock artist who tiptoes into country waters, like Bon Jovi. A traditional country fan may like these artists, but he might not readily acknowledge them as bona-fide country performers. Yet to a rock fan, they become as country as Garth Brooks.

That is not to say a rock fan would ignore a more traditional act such as Alan Jackson. He is just more likely to gravitate to an edgier artist like Steve Earle. The influx of rock fans does not make it easier for Alan Jackson to have a mass appeal hit. Alan will still encounter the same hurdles in reaching crossover audiences.

In order to become that mass appeal hit, the song must hit many genres. For Alan Jackson, that included making a dance remix of the song, "Good Time." Rather than the straight album version, he added electronic drumbeats to young women line dancing in the video. At its core, the song remained country, with the fiddle as prominent as in the original. But the added dance touch made it far more accessible to a new, younger audience.

Shakira's "Hips Don't Lie" is the perfect example of a song that really went out of its way to contain elements of multiple genres. At its heart, it is a clear and simple pop song. The rhythms, however, are club oriented, and lean toward Latin beats, specifically a light version of Reggaeton. Producer Wyclef Jean's intro and brief raps, accented with a sample from the classic hip-hop anthem "Déjà Vu (Uptown Baby)," tie her neatly into the hip-hop world. Put it all together, and you no longer hit just one element of Shakira's fan base, but nearly every potential fan. With no other songs exploiting these relationships to this degree, "Hips Don't Lie" easily became the most-played song of 2006.

In today's music business, being the most-played song at radio does not guarantee sales revenue any longer. As Internet airplay revenue grows in importance, achieving high airplay levels online, as opposed to on radio, will also grow. These multiple-genre touch points that lead to additional play events will also become the subtle elements that generate increased revenues. Naturally, this will also cause these songs to climb the charts faster. Wide audience potential gives these songs the edge over those that stick to just one genre. That edge might only be a small percentage, but they can also mean several thousand dollars in revenue and a higher chart berth.

CHART POSITIONING

These chart positions have always been important to gauge a measure of the song's success. The future will likely be no different, and might actually be more important. In the past decade, the charts were mostly based on radio formats. The mass appeal *Billboard* Hot 100 became less influential, while the top-selling album charts became very volatile. Labels concerned themselves more with a strong opening week than long-term sales. Charts, therefore, became individual ghettos. Most people view only the chart that pertains to the musical style that relates to them. It was not about figuring out what had the most appeal, but rather how to have the broadest reach with a niche appeal.

The charts, though, were solely based on radio airplay. As this airplay continues to diminish, the charts need to rely more on those services that generate listening events. That will come from a multitude of online sites, and their much more varied approaches to playing music. These approaches often disregard genre, and focus more on popularity and/or individual musical tastes. This makes continuing genre-based charts a logistical nightmare, and an inaccurate reflection of the true reach of a song.

The accurate reflections of the marketplace will likely shift back to the *Billboard* Hot 100 and other like-minded charts that refuse to break out song airplay based on any one genre. These charts will also gain in importance as an accurate reflection of the song's approximate gross revenue, much like a box-office chart. As sales become only one portion of the revenue equation, the chart of tomorrow will likely take into account all potential experiential and purchasable revenue streams. This includes sales (physical and digital), partial sales (ringtones and other experiential song usages), and airplay (along with subsequent royalties).

This new future chart now serves an additional purpose. It helps gauge a song's potential revenue. This allows for a more accurate accounting of sound recording revenues than has ever been achieved before. It also gives a much truer picture of a song's national popularity than has ever been achieved. This makes the chart more relevant to other areas where popularity is crucial, including decisions made by music supervisors or Top Forty programmers who need to be mass appeal by definition.

The lack of viability in fragmented format charts also makes positioning on the overall chart more important than ever. In a given week, the most popular major music formats are broken out into ten charts. This means the Top Forty chart could potentially contain 400 songs that are given exposure to varying degrees, though it would not likely reach this number, as many songs appear on multiple charts.

If only one chart became the industry standard, only forty songs could achieve significant industry visibility. The scarcity of chart positioning would increase competition, as the number of titles balloons to unsustainable proportions. Songs are going to need the dramatic edges detailed here to better guarantee chart positioning. Such edges can determine the difference between number forty-one and forty, which can mean everything to that song's visibility.

In order to satisfy such tight competition, chart compilers will need to try to rely on a few guidelines, such as blocking any one artist from having multiple songs on the chart. An artist with simultaneous hits could and should happen again, for hype like that helped elevate the Beatles to near-sainthood in the 1960s. But the practice will likely be discouraged to insure that more artists have the opportunity to experience success. While the charts will ultimately not be able to fully control this, it will be an element they regularly monitor for a fair and balanced chart.

One area the chart can monitor is having the same song in multiple chart positions. To make sure that the chart has forty distinct songs in the Top Forty, remixes and live versions, which ostensibly could get significant play on their own, would likely be rolled up into one chart listing. The need for this rollup and the diversity in the charts will ultimately give song makers one more trick in the arsenal to insure they release a successful song.

9

MULTIPLE VERSIONS

Currently, when a radio station plays a song in any form, the radio monitoring services count each play under one listing: The original song title. That means if the station plays a remix, a live version, or any other iteration of the song that exists, it all counts as airplay of the base song. These additional versions do not really juice up the charts that much, and are usually put into rotation to keep things fresh on the airwaves. The song would likely have seen nearly identical play counts whether the different versions existed or not. Exceptions might be dance-based shows, where remixes would likely be incremental airplay above normal rotation. The importance of multiple versions will grow substantially in the next few years, and it actually starts with the restrictions placed on songs.

DMCA LOOPHOLE

The Digital Millennium Copyright Act, or DMCA, placed limitations on what a digital broadcaster could play and when. Much of the DMCA does not apply to airplay itself. The parts that do apply establish crucial criteria that make it difficult for digital broadcasters to achieve individual song impressions akin to terrestrial radio. The main tenet is that broadcasters are allowed to play only a maximum of four songs from any one artist within a three-hour period. While those four songs technically could be the same song four times in that three-hour period, most services observe the law's intention that the songs are different sound recordings. With that, any one single song is highly unlikely to receive multiple impressions within one set listening experience.

This restriction was implemented at a time when airplay on Top Forty radio dramatically increased. At their peak, songs played every sixty minutes. Furthermore, in the late 1990s, the length of time songs stayed on the air in current rotation was also dramatically increasing. This made radio playlists difficult to infiltrate from labels of any size. Limiting airplay on digital outlets was a strategy that satisfied labels that wanted more "slots" for their artists' music, and artist rights' advocates who viewed radio playlists as repetitive and restrictive.

The question became how a digital radio station could insure compliance while offering unique features and programming, much of which is automated. The answer, oddly enough, is that some programmers had to consider restrictions that are deeper than what the DMCA required. The danger in violating the DMCA rules amounted to increased costs in the form of lawsuits and/or higher royalty rates for the violating company, neither of which was desirable. This became especially true a few years after the DMCA passage, when the fabled dot-com bust made penny pinching a new religion.

Simultaneously, online radio outlets wanted to make a distinctly different product than terrestrial radio, so it was actually advantageous to have these restrictions. To gain new audience share, these outlets had to attract people who were disgruntled with the repetitive playlists that permeate radio stations. The easiest way to do that was to offer more diversity in the song offerings and much lower repetition. By logging into the radio service, stations track personalized radio streams and airplay across multiple stations and sessions to further insure a lack of repetition. So if you listen to "Hips Don't Lie" in one two-hour session on Monday and do not listen again until Thursday, the system is unlikely to repeat the song three days later. Even with the song's popularity and likely inclusion in the playlist, the system may still view the song as having played more recently than other hits, especially against a likely database of millions of potential songs.

These checks and balances insure DMCA compliancy above and beyond the stated boundaries. It also makes song repetition more difficult to achieve for any individual. This is not a big concern for digital broadcasters, but now that online airplay has come into its own, and this airplay can generate promotion, chart position, and income, the artist and label community will become anxious. Digital broadcasters, even with label pressures, are unlikely to change their programming models drastically. The product differentiation to terrestrial radio is too important. The restrictions have also become infrastructure at these outlets, making change within them a difficult proposition. Plus, these companies pay for this airplay, and will likely not let the label payees dictate how to spend their royalty budget.

The inclusion of multiple versions of each individual song, especially as that song ascends to hit status, is going to become a strong tool. The obvious usage will be an extension of the methods that radio currently uses alternate versions. A rock song would never fit in well on a dance station. The dance remix would. In terrestrial radio, this extra bump for a dance remix would occur infrequently, most often on a weekend evening during a "dance party" specialty show. Online, airplay of this version could potentially occur at all hours of the day, any day. These airplay events would not be limited to the specialty hours, but would occur whenever the user wanted to listen to that particular station.

Inclusion in these stations would also open up that song to a whole new listener base, thereby exposing it to people who might have never heard the original version. As detailed in the last chapter, users are more likely to be more open to songs of other genres. With that, they are also more open to embracing these songs as part of their permanent collection than in years past. These listeners might not tune into that dance party, for example, when traditional radio offered it. All of a sudden, a song that would not have been on a listener's radar becomes an integral title. Just as crucial, the song generates money from a consumer who heretofore had been untapped.

The clearest reason why multiple versions will be successful lies in the DMCA rules. In general, label metadata delineates each individual version of a song as a unique title with its own identifier, called an ISRC code. For various purposes, any version that deviates has a different set of metadata, and is therefore a different song. To a database, something as distinct as a "clean" version and a "dirty" version of any particular song are as different as Cher's "I Got You Babe" and "Believe." It does not matter that the root song title is the same. The difference in the version changes it to a completely different set of metadata.

What this means for services with personalization elements is dramatic. These engines are looking for similarities. So, using "Hips Don't Lie" as an example, when the engine looks to see if someone bought and/or liked the song, it will also check to see what other songs the consumer bought or liked, and discover similarities to create recommendations. Generally, only a small minority of the audience will yield the top nexus in song similarity. It is doubtful that 50% of "Hips Don't Lie" fans will also like any one particular song in unison.

Except for...alternate versions of "Hips Don't Lie." These recommendation engines will find that small portions of the audience also like particular tracks. In the case of Shakira, that would be other pop hits from the time, such as Nelly Furtado's "Promiscuous," Rihanna's "Unfaithful," and Gnarls Barkley's "Crazy." But these recommendations are easily trumped by alternate versions of the same song, if they exist in these systems. It is not easy to dispute that people who like "Hips Don't Lie" will also like "Hips Don't Lie." It is akin to saying people who like apples also like apples. The root of it is that people who like Red Delicious apples also have a high probability of liking Golden Delicious apples, or even Granny Smith apples. There are differences to be sure, but it is still an easy judgment call.

ROLLUPS

So with those similarities firmly in place, these obvious recommendations then begin to occur throughout each system, including sites that sell music. These can potentially upsell fans who might purchase two or three versions instead of one. This can happen either accidentally (someone purchases the alternate version instead of the official one), or on purpose (the fan needs to collect all iterations). At the end, all versions roll up into the master-title listing on the tracking service SoundScan. An extreme case occurred in 2006 when Epic Records released 500 "personalized" versions of the Jessica Simpson song, "A Public Affair," for sale on Yahoo! The resulting additional sales gave the track a boost that vaulted it into the top ten download sales, while it would have been number twelve without the benefit of the additional versions.

On radio services, additional versions may work around internal DMCA safeguards just enough to nudge a few multiple impressions into the mix. On personalized services, when the user identifies the original version as something he likes, the service will immediately look for similar songs and likely find the alternate versions. Since both DMCA and internal programming restrictions would likely hold back the original version from airplay, the alternate version would subsequently play at a later period, most likely prior to the point where the service would have played the original version for a second time.

Yet some programmed stations do not have filters that increase or decrease airplay for particular songs. Others offer a limited playlist, where the song order is randomly generated. If the playlist has 100 songs in it, then there is a 1% chance that the song in question will actually play in any given moment. If, however, an alternate version is also created and placed within the same playlist, that song would then have a 2% chance of being played. A small number to be sure, but a 100% increase—along with this repeating over multiple sites--could result in a dramatic increase in plays that would be noticeable both on airplay charts and on royalty statements.

MUSIC VIDEOS

Music videos will also be affected by multiple versions. This time, the rules are different, as the DMCA does not specifically cover music videos, and therefore most of the airplay is handled by direct label licenses not necessarily covered by the DMCA rules. Traditionally, music videos are considered a one-to-one relationship, whereby one video is created, and remains the only visual representation available for that particular song.

Videos were initially created almost solely for airplay on MTV. There was little need for multiple versions, as the channel played only one version, and seldom stuck with any one particular song for a long enough period that the original version would burn out. Other uses, such as clubs, local shows, and home video would only have minimal impact, and therefore were marginalized. During the 1980s, when the format was still burgeoning and people were figuring out the rules, programmers experimented with multiple versions in these marginalized outlets, most often with no incremental impact. In the 1990s, as MTV became essentially the only outlet, and production expenses for the average video rose from five to six figures, the labels kept costs in control by making only one version—the MTV-approved one.

The rules changed dramatically at the turn of the twenty-first century. One label that started breaking the rules early was Warner Bros. Records. The company knew it was a challenge to place developing artists on MTV. It was also forward-thinking in seeing the impact that the Internet could have at developing fan bases for these new artists, and creating the story that television would eventually notice. To this end, in 2003, it made a relatively inexpensive version of a new artist's video, such as My Chemical Romance's "I'm Not Okay (I Promise)," and released it online. Other models followed. The low budget was balanced by either creativity or basic visuals that served to expose the artists' image. When the online push successfully sold records, Warner Bros. made a second video for the same song with normal budgets. That version was the one that eventually made its way onto MTV. Online, however, both versions continued to co-exist. The new video brought established fans back to watch new visuals from an already identified favorite song. Meanwhile, new fans watched the old video to devour all available content from that artist. The resulting lift brought these titles to greater viewership than previously achieved. It also resulted in higher chart positioning on these sites, thereby bolstering the developing story needed to push MTV, radio stations, and retail stores into action.

These reactions to multiple versions were basically unintended side effects to the larger purpose of breaking a new artist. Video royalties had yet to be established, and online video outlets had just begun reporting airplay to Broadcast Data Systems. Now that the environment has been established, the potential for additional exploitations with multiple versions also grows. The obvious one, already explored, is the rollup of these versions into one BDS listing that will affect charts. These versions would differ by the visuals, not the audio, so all the impressions are of the original version of the song, instead of the alternate versions previously discussed. Adding up all of these versions will result in higher chart positioning, and the appearance of larger success of that particular song.

User generated videos also exponentially increase the number of versions and the impact they have on the song's overall success and royalties. Similarity recommendations will highlight these multiple versions, regularly drawing additional song activity. The success of the new versions may also keep the song visible on top charts after the original version wanes in popularity.

The overall viewing behavior of the music consumer is unlikely to change from the beginning of online video. New and old fans will move total airplay numbers up or down, depending on when these titles are released. This will result in multiple strategies for hit making from record labels. This can include:

- Releasing multiple versions at once to drive multiple views from single individuals that create dramatic spikes in chart position.
- Closely timed releases of different versions to further momentum of a song both within public consciousness, as well as chart positioning.
- Spreading out multiple versions over longer periods of time to allow buildup of a developing story, and/or to coincide with promotion to varied audiences.

Any and all of these strategies, when timed correctly and fully learned and understood by label marketing departments, will easily result in effective strategies in breaking a particular song.

The environment has changed so dramatically in recent years that it is not just about the chart game. Royalty payments for videos are now generating revenues from a format that previously had been solely promotional in nature. When these new lower-budget videos become successful, they can be profitable just through online airplay from the major outlets. Videos are now both a promotional tool and a profit center.

Multiple versions of the same video will become the quickest and easiest way to make those titles profitable. This will most often occur via editing. Taking a cue from major movie studios, labels will make more music videos available in a variety of formats. Some will contain content that conforms to an "artist's true vision," while others may be more risqué. In these scenarios, the editing for content required for television becomes an asset, instead of a liability. Most often these edits are shots of weapons, but can also be sexually suggestive shots of females in various stages of undress. Websites, under much less scrutiny than TV networks, have more leeway to accept these images, especially when they can sit side-by-side with the MTV edit as a "Director's Cut."

The cheapest multiple versions an artist can make are the ones created by the fans. This is organically happening on video-sharing sites, but the use could be encouraged. If the labels gave fans materials such as raw footage, photos, or other images, along with their support, more videos would be created. This, in turn, would lead to more versions that ultimately collect royalties on these sites. Similarly, the affordability of these cuts could easily lead to artists and labels hiring people to create their own videos that give the appearance of being user generated.

Additional cuts can extend a video further by offering more of a story or a much longer version of the video. This can include scripted set-ups, story-based interludes, or other devices that can take the length of the video far beyond the actual song length. Since television often has to keep videos to the shortest length possible to maximize the most musical entertainment per second, most artists have avoided these devices in their videos. The Internet now allows this creativity to flourish. The caveat is that these videos traditionally have a much higher skip rate than a normal video. They can expand the audience, but should not be used as the primary video, as they will likely generate fewer BDS plays and subsequently fewer royalties.

The "multiple ending" video will also be used more often. Since only the last few seconds of the video need to change, this allows another cheap, effective way to maximize video play. The viewer has to wait until the end of the video to see the subtle difference from other versions, thus virtually guaranteeing that these versions will receive higher BDS plays than other "multiple version" concepts. More versions will also lead to more BDS plays from individual fans, and it all leads to higher royalties. It is unlikely that these will receive large plays over long periods. But these manipulations can be enough to garner necessary play and royalty bumps to make their contribution in the hit making process a necessity. It is also likely that this particular idea will have a quicker burnout factor. Yet that can likely take many years, so this idea should be effective for quite awhile.

A different take on that same theme is the video that tells a story in multiple parts, but uses the same song. In essence, the video could be a fifteen to twenty-minute film when all is said and done. But with the video being told in four to six different parts, people feel obligated to tune in to find out what happens next. The most extreme, yet groundbreaking example is R. Kelly's urban saga, "Trapped In The Closet." The initial output of this concept went twelve parts deep, and told a soap opera story through song and video. Granted, the lyrics changed for each part of the song. But it was a bold move and proved that a very simple and inexpensive idea could easily result in new untapped revenue sources. The resounding buzz also created a significant chart lift for R. Kelly, as well.

Another revival will be more R-rated videos appearing in various sources online. In the infancy of music videos, nudity was used to create cheap buzz around artists, and the attention-grabbing stunts in this new format often were very effective. This was first successful in the original version of Duran Duran's early video, "Girls On Film," which featured nude and scantily clad models, replete with overt sexual overtones, fighting in a boxing ring. Since then, nudity has been used regularly, but sparingly, i.e. an eyebrow-raising stunt with resulting PR (Madonna's "Justify My Love"), an underground buzzmaker for industry tastemakers (Nelly's

"Tipdrill"), and even an artistic statement (the Prodigy's "Smack My Bitch Up"). Each example had its own purpose, but with the exception of Madonna, who sold a lot of video singles, the videos themselves were rarely seen.

The Internet and the ready availability of porn has made it easier to find and view these videos. Even though they are largely tame compared to most pornography found online, they satisfy an inherent desire from consumers to see music stars and their songs married to R-rated content. However, these titles will not generate additional chart buzz, because the major sites will be unlikely to carry them. While their standards are more relaxed than broadcast television, they are owned by publicly traded companies who must uphold to obvious moral standards.

Where these videos will be seen, though, is on other sites that feature this specific type of content. Labels will likely look to these sites for royalties that are a percentage of revenue, rather than a per-play model. In order to protect views by underage users, these sites will need to charge a nominal fee. The bigger revenue would be from the percentage of this fee, instead of each individual play. Since the number of titles is a much smaller pool to choose from (few artists can actually make these videos, given their public image), the revenue per play will likely be higher than on mainstream sites. The resulting figure would be a decent revenue generator. Meanwhile, general awareness of the content's existence will also result in increased airplay for the "PG-13" version that appears on mainstream sites. Many people would likely view this version thinking they were getting the more explicit edit. It may even be satisfactory for some viewers.

Any of these versions derive their biggest benefit by having the only additional expense in the editing. Once the principal photography has been completed, the editor can take all of the footage and put it into any number of versions the artist and record company desires. This cost would add only a few thousand dollars to the overall budget.

Meanwhile, additional revenues derived from the multiple versions of a hit song could easily hit the tens of thousands, not to mention additional revenues the song would receive from the visibility of a higher chart position.

Doing it on the cheap is not the only option a record label has. It can also make a more expensive video around entirely new concepts. This will likely lead to less profitability, but a new big budget concept would generate the highest number of multiple views. Users will gravitate more easily to a visual that has a distinctly different look than other videos that have similar structures.

Live videos can also be a decent way to add additional visibility of a song, and showcase the performance chops of the artist as well. Most major online outlets record several acts in their own studio for exclusive purposes. These outlets are much more apt to promote these titles, and this leads to more marketing support, along with increased airplay and visibility for the original title. Historically, these types of videos perform poorly compared to their concept-created counterparts, but the lower costs generally offset the performance numbers to make it a worthwhile consideration.

Additional versions such as these also allow record labels to deliver more "exclusives" to multiple sites. Before the Internet, labels mostly went to MTV for "exclusive premiere" positioning. They never worried about losing other opportunities, because there were few alternatives. With the Internet, this has changed dramatically, with several outlets providing significant benefits to a video premiere. MTV still rolls out a big bang, but Yahoo! Music has also delivered a premiere platform with numbers that rival those of a television network. iTunes offers video premieres as a purchase, and serves up larger revenue opportunities than any other outlet, even if the total viewership is smaller. Other national outlets, ranging from AOL and MSN to MySpace and YouTube, also provide substantial platforms for a video debut, and viable niche sites will likely spring up in the future.

What ultimately generates the large airplay numbers from those premiere promotions is the surrounding marketing that goes into the premiere itself. If a record label chooses one broadcaster over the others, that broadcaster guarantees significant placement throughout its platforms. This, however, comes at the expense of similar promotions on other outlets. In fact, other outlets may hold back promotional opportunities for that artist if they feel slighted. That could negatively affect revenues and sales. The parsing out of multiple video versions allows for a much greater potential that more than one outlet will provide marketing support, which leads to greater airplay and chart positioning. These outlets might also make available more than one version, though their exclusive would get all the promotion. When viewers then explore to find the additional versions, it increases all the metrics.

Once again, the user who invests in all these versions becomes someone who feels indebted to the song. Watching multiple versions of the song will lead to multiple impressions of the song. At a time when getting any listener to hear a song more than once becomes increasingly difficult, any tactic to hook multiple listens is a welcome one, as it will lock in familiarity over time. Once a user gets locked into checking out the varied versions of a video, there will exist a certain guilt factor, and missing a version could mean losing out on a vital part of the artist's expression. Though there will likely be a limit to how many "versions" a fan can accept before that guilt wears off, it should last through enough versions to make the song familiar.

With multiple versions getting increased attention across multiple music sites, many ancillary opportunities will blossom, including blogs, message boards, tagging, and news sites. All of these popular interconnected links will also lead to increased positioning on search engines. These will likely make the video links more visible on simple searches for the artist or song, thereby leading to potential views. The diversity of the titles will also lead to more choices from within the search results itself. This can lead to a user going back to the results and clicking on more than one link, again likely leading to increased usage and consistent prominent search placement.

None of these new versions will make a user watch any more music videos than he would have. If he were planning on watching videos for an hour, he will unlikely extend that hour just to fit in two extra versions of an artist's video. Instead, a more likely scenario is that the user will not view other artists' videos that he might otherwise have seen. Once again, the underlying benefit is boxing out the competition and their potential for views, chart position, and royalties. This benefit is increasingly important as video becomes an accepted part of viewing time on the Internet, cell phones, and video iPods, alongside television. Music video time is also being eroded by home videos, news content, video games, user-generated content, and other entertainment videos from traditional outlets. The time users spend watching videos will be even more limited as the pull from other types of content grows stronger. Making sure these users watch the videos of one artist over another is of paramount importance to financial and chart success.

All this additional activity makes multiple versions, whether in audio or video form, an important weapon in a song's domination of the heart and mind of the music consumer. With an artist needing to release more songs more often to keep a fan base engaged, these versions must come swiftly and decisively for maximum effectiveness. If the versions are done correctly, the resulting multiple listens will create familiarity that leaves the listener singing that song for many years to come. But are multiple impressions enough of a guarantee that the listener will remember? With all the demands on people's time, even a few repeated listens may not be enough. For any one artist, this can especially be true when he is releasing product at a fast clip in order to keep the fan base engaged. To truly secure that hit in the listener's mind, and to make sure it sticks quickly and efficiently, repetition has to come from within. In other words, the song itself needs to make the listener feel as if multiple repetitions have already occurred. To do that, the industry will resort to a tried-and-true technique that will make a much more common appearance than in years past.

10

REPEAT WITHIN A SONG

Music programmers at radio stations are notorious for making snap judgments on songs. The reason is that actual music programming makes up only one part of their workweek. Piles of music from multiple record companies, managers and artists have to be listened to in an efficient manner. Often the programmer has time only to listen to a portion of the dozens of songs submitted weekly and make a snap decision based on what he hears. This method is not the ideal way for a programmer to listen to music. But he wants to be fair to as many people as possible.

When the programmer hears songs in that fashion, it is common for him to forget them, especially ones he did not like. They often blur together, especially when many songs share the same production values to conform to the radio format's "sound." When the record companies calls the programmer to ask what he thinks of the song, there is always a possibility he will not remember unless he took notes. No matter how big a music fan he is, remembering individual songs can be a daunting task. About all he can adequately remember is if a song grabbed him with extreme emotional power (which is rare), or if the song is programmed ad nauseum in heavy rotation on his station (which is often).

Consumers rarely had to worry about such troubles. Very few had the disposable income to spend the hundreds of dollars it would require to actually obtain and own that many songs per week. Those who did have the money seldom had the time to embrace all those songs to their fullest extent. Only an extremely small cadre of music junkies could remember that many songs. The majority of consumers would get exposed to only a small set of new songs per week, which was limited to what was played on the radio or on television. What they would purchase to listen to on their own schedule was an even smaller set. While not ideal from a business perspective, this arrangement suited consumers just fine. Not being exposed to a whole world of music due to tight radio playlists and inconvenient purchasing economics was just not a cause for alarm.

FILE TRADING

In the beginning of the twenty-first century, digital technology took this arrangement and upended it. The first wave came through illicit digital distribution, beginning with Napster. No longer constrained to what was on a retail shelf or what one could afford, people began consuming significantly larger amounts of new music on a regular basis. For music junkies, this meant exploring rare, hard-to-find titles that had eluded them. For most people who downloaded, this just meant obtaining every possible song they could think of at any point.

In only a couple of years, these programs became easier to use. While file swapping on sites like Limewire and Kazaa grabbed many of the headlines, millions of music consumers also moved to BitTorrent, which allows a faster transfer of large files, as a preferred distribution method. Unlike most file-sharing services, which employ computers communicating one-on-one, BitTorrent breaks the file (called a torrent) into pieces which are then downloaded via multiple computers around the world. Very quickly, downloading became less about hunting for individual songs and more about obtaining and listening to whole catalogs. A user would not just download Led Zeppelin's "Stairway to Heaven." He would download the entire Led Zeppelin catalog in a matter of hours. And he would not just download one or two big hits. He would download a torrent called "Top 40 Hits" that contained *all* of the songs in the current pop chart. Very quickly, these music fans had the ability to listen to a large quantity of songs and then filter to a manageable amount on their own.

The second breakthrough came with the nature of music distribution itself. Prior to the Internet, releasing your own records was mostly a vanity project. Vinyl was expensive and cumbersome to produce, as was the CD in its early days. Additional hurdles occurred with major labels creating a virtual hammerlock on music retail, making it harder for an artist to stock the music to sell. Even if the artist managed to convince a retailer to sell his music, it often would be difficult to find in the store. Then, if by some miracle the music did sell, the retailer would seldom pay for the product. His priorities were paying the rent, utilities, and employees. The major labels that shipped the retailer lots of releases got paid far faster than the independent artist. Screwing the little guy was rarely a concern, as there was seldom any significant recourse the artist could take.

The Internet quickly changed things, as there are now easy ways for artists to go around these gatekeepers. Artists can establish a one-to-one relationship with their fans and sell directly. Going even further, a company called CD Baby formed to aggregate tens of thousands of independently released titles in one convenient marketplace, and others followed suit soon after. For a nominal fee, any artist could make his music available for sale to anyone, anywhere in the world. At the same time, CD plants brought down the manufacturing costs of a CD to around a dollar. Furthermore, CD burners became standard in computers, and a musician with time on his hands could make as many copies of his music as he wanted to right in his home.

THE VOLUME PROBLEM

The resulting explosion of artistic expression was staggering. Between the years 2000 and 2005, the number of full-length CD releases reportedly doubled from 30,000 titles to 60,000. The majority of those titles were of the homegrown variety, and over 75% of them never even managed to sell 100 copies. Nevertheless, the opportunity for the music to be heard spurred musicians to create and distribute like they never had before.

The end game became more about being heard than about selling product. Sites like MySpace and PureVolume made it extremely easy for artists to upload and distribute streams of their music. Social networking made it even easier for potential fans to discover the music, and for the artists to communicate with those fans. Add file trading and torrent sites to the mix, and significant audiences now heard many of these artists, even if official sales tallies may not have been commensurate to total listens.

A wealth of musical riches was now available to the average music listener. But time became an enemy. The day still contained only twenty-four hours, so it was physically possible to listen to only 5% of all recorded music released in a year, and that was only if the listener never slept. Along with music, other entertainment began competing fiercely for that time. Video games rose in popularity, drawing many people into hours of focused usage. Communications took on a whole new level with email, followed by instant messaging, and then mobile text messaging. Suddenly, communicating with friends became a full-time job. Even the definition of "friend" changed, as MySpace instilled the notion that a small, core group of friends may not be enough. All these factors come on top of the "normal" everyday time spent on school, work, and family, and take chunks of time out of a person's day.

The large influx of music colliding with greater demands on people's time created a listening atmosphere for consumers that is very similar to that of radio programmers. Now, the average music listener does not have time to waste on a song unworthy of his time. As previously discussed, these users will give a song only seven seconds or so before they skip to something else. If anything, radio programmers usually wait a minute for the hook to show up before they move on, but they get paid to do that. The average consumer does not feel that giving a song a chance is a right or an obligation. The fact that these same users multitask while listening also means that less attention is paid to the music itself.

As with radio programmers, this often means that music fans do not remember what songs they hear. It is also fairly common for consumers to forget they even own a song, downloading it a second or third time if some conversation, blog, or other factor sparks an interest at that moment. Great songs are often overlooked just because the listener has only so big an attention span at any one given time.

The consumer also has no greater capacity to remember songs. The human brain is still intrinsically the same, so the average music consumer does not have the ability to remember a larger number of songs than he did a decade ago. If anything, the capacity may be diminished because of all the additional demands on the listener's time.

All of this poses a problem in making a song memorable and lasting to the listener. The songs that truly become profitable over time are the ones that become an indelible part of a listener's life. This only gets achieved through multiple impressions of that song to firmly establish it as a lasting track. As multiple impressions become an increasingly rare occurrence, it becomes imperative upon the songwriter to employ as many techniques as possible to make that song memorable.

SINGABILITY

What gives a song its permanence is almost always the ease in which the listener can sing it. At a live concert, when a familiar song is played, it is rare that the audience is quiet. A large portion of the audience is almost certain to sing along. In fact, the singer usually encourages this through a variety of techniques that engage the audience and make their communal singing a part of the show. It also goes a long way to reinforce that song within that audience.

Once a song is easily sung, it becomes a lot easier for the listener to remember it. The trick is how to achieve that in one listen. The devices are similar to other techniques of memory retention. For example, many experts recommend upon meeting a person for the first time, one should use the name of the person he has met in conversation as many times as possible. The theory goes the more the name is actually spoken, the more likely it will be remembered. One can say that just being told the person's name should be enough to remember it, but this is seldom true. Actually speaking the name increases the chances the name will be retained.

Much like meeting someone you may never see again, the first listen of a song may be the only listen unless the songwriter compels someone to listen again. The more the listener can be inspired to sing even a small portion of the song, the more likely he will listen to that song again.

THE CHORUS

Placing the chorus at the beginning of a song is helpful to start that process, but it may not be enough to engage the listener. The hook at the beginning may ensnare a person to listen to the entire song, but that does not guarantee that he will walk away with the song in his memory. If the listener does not easily sing that early placement of the hook, it will not lead to a repeat listen.

It may feel like appealing to a lowest common denominator, but one of the best things the performer and songwriter can do is utilize repetition as much as possible. By repeating the memorable portions of the song, you will dramatically increase the likelihood that the listener will inevitably begin repeating those words. This repetition can occur with prolonged choruses at various portions of the song. Another technique can be to gradually increase the length of the repetitive portions (likely the chorus) as the song progresses.

Increasing repetition at the end of the song will likely make the listener remember it. This is not a new technique by any means. It really came into its own after singles began running longer than three minutes. A prolonged end chorus both extended the song to an acceptable length that befits a hit song, and also made the song more memorable. Utilizing a previous example, Adam Ant's "Goody Two Shoes" deviated from the fairly standard practice of repeating a chorus twice at the end of the song. Instead, the chorus was repeated five times and made up the final fifty-three seconds of the song. To put it bluntly, one-fourth of the song is nothing but the end chorus. On paper, it may seem trite and dull. In delivery, it made for a memorable hit.

Hanging the chorus at the beginning of the song would cause most performers to simply adjust a song so that the initial chorus, in effect, becomes a "bonus" chorus. If this is the only major change to a song, the end results are significant. The song starts immediately, grabs the listener with the hook, adds an additional repetition of the chorus to make it memorable, and also elongates the song by as much as thirty seconds. All of these things subtly increase the dominance of that song in generating chart positioning and royalties. While this would not work for all songs, this simple change has a dramatic potential that easily outstrips the technique's simplicity.

Another way to establish the chorus throughout the song is by taking its elements and placing them in the background throughout the verses. This can be achieved through countermelodies that are not prominently heard in the mix, or literal background singers. Their placement can be subtle enough that the chorus takes on a larger degree of familiarity without the listener realizing how that happened.

If lyrically placing the chorus in the background of a verse does not work, allusions to the melody line may be enough to add sonic reinforcing. Film composers often add a lot of illusory techniques to their scores. They emphasize which characters and feelings are present at a particular moment. While the cues are often dramatically different, the allusions are there to strike subtle familiarity without being in the foreground. Adding those melody lines where plausible within the body of a song can achieve that same effect. Its subtlety heightens the impact and can prove tremendously helpful, especially if repeating the chorus too much is not an option for a particular song.

An additional technique is the increased usage of choruses sung by a literal chorus of people. By adding multiple singers and/or a multi-tracked vocal line to the same melody line (and not necessarily harmonies), the producer creates the desired effect that a song is already familiar, even if the listener is hearing it for the first time. When a person hears a group of people singing along, it adds to his ability to embrace and sing along with the song, as well.

In general, singing along does not come naturally to most people. Singing solo, as any singer can tell you, is usually a gutsy move that requires a lot of confidence. If a wrong note is sung while the singer is in the spotlight, the blame can only be placed on the individual singer. Singing in a group, however, usually masks the imperfections of those whose techniques are not as strong, or who do not wish to be showy, or just tend to shy away from the spotlight. To coax these people to sing, the vocals of the group must be strong enough that the individual singer can be comfortable being a part of it.

The argument can be made that recorded music is not specifically about singing—that it is actually about listening. This does have credence, but placing emphasis on that makes the music too passive to engage the listener. The act of singing the song increases the chances that the song will be memorable to the listener. Once again, much like repeating a person's name to remember it, getting a person to sing the song will insure it has a longer and more extensive shelf life. Even repeating this technique in this chapter causes the reader to remember it, so the same can be done for the song itself.

SIMULATING THE GROUP EXPERIENCE

The catch is that the majority of devices that people now use to listen to music are not conducive to group experiences. For many people, the computer has replaced the home stereo. Individual computer speakers without much power have replaced big speakers that could be heard all over the house. Headphones and ear buds are used far more often. iPods and other portable digital players isolate by requiring headphones to experience the music. Even though people can hear music broadly from an iPod in home speaker systems, cars, and bars, their usage is generally much lower than headphone listening. The portable device is thought of as an individual experience that isolates the person from the world, thereby increasing solo listening experiences. The act of web surfing is rarely physically communal, so most songs heard online are for an audience of one. While sharing these songs is prevalent and does expose them to more people, they are not heard simultaneously in the same physical space. This severely diminishes the chances that a group of people would sing the song.

With a high likelihood of an isolated listening experience, it's incumbent upon artists, musicians, and producers to adapt the songs so the solo listener will sing along. Adding a chorus of people singing the hooks makes the listener feel as if he's listening to a group. This increases the likelihood that he, himself, will sing along. In recent years, a micro-trend sprung up in which choruses are shouted as a chant rather than sung. Gwen Stefani popularized this with "Hollaback Girl," and Fergie followed suit the following year with "London Bridge." These songs gained popularity quickly because listeners did not even have to learn the notes or worry about being off-key. They just had to learn the playground-like chants that instantly made them more accessible.

Along the same lines, call-and-response techniques also work to establish familiarity. Historically, this has always been an effective way to both engage an audience and get it to learn the song. The call-and-response practice dates back to African tribes. There, a leader would sing the line to a song, and the rest of the tribe would respond, often with the same line. As Africans spread around the world, so did the technique. Religions adopted call-and-response techniques for prayers to insure that parishioners would remember them. In recorded music, call-and-response was originally found in gospel, blues, and jazz. As rock music evolved from these forms, rock musicians also placed call-and-response into their songs, though sparingly. Over the years, call-and-response has been utilized by artists of all stripes in the live experience, yet shows up less often in recent recorded works.

This will likely change as more techniques are needed to make songs more easily sung. As with chorusing, a strategically placed call-and-response in a song will subconsciously force the listener to take part in that song. This will then mentally connect the listener and the song.

The call-and-response can take place in a couple of ways. One is in a very traditional sense. The singer will sing a line from a portion of the song, most likely the chorus, and a choir of singers will then sing it in return. If this is done quickly and often enough, the listener will likely find himself singing (or thinking of singing) the chorused part, whether he wants to or not.

Another technique is to have a particular line sung throughout the song by a chorus, which punctuates a variety of lyrics. These lyrics can take place in the chorus, verse, bridge, or even all three. This requires that the listener needs only to remember one line, as opposed to repeating several lines utilizing other call-and-response techniques. If done right, that phrase would likely be repeated far more often within the body of the song than just a standard call-and-response. This allows for more impressions of the hook, and again helps the song stick in the memory of the listener.

A great example of this technique appears in Randy Newman's "I Love L.A." Throughout the song, a group chants the words, "We love it!" after nearly every single line in both the bridge and the chorus. Newman even overemphasizes this in the last bridge. Instead of chanting the line once, the choir chants it six times. That is more than half of the eleven times the phrase is chanted in the song. Having the chant begin with "we" further allows the song to bond with the listener. The group is part of that collective "we," and the feeling of belonging makes remembering the song much easier. Even though Randy has had a prolific, critically acclaimed career for over forty years, "I Love L.A." is probably the one Randy Newman song that casual music fans can easily sing at a the drop of a hat. This is a testament to the power of the call-and-response in creating that familiarity.

If an artist is ambitious enough, he can create more subtle deceit by establishing the call-and-response and then take it away. If the response lines are strong enough, many producers may opt *out* of including the actual response line when it is delivered late in the song. Much like the incomplete ending discussed in Chapter Five, taking the line out of the song practically forces the listener to fill in the gap. If done at the very end, the abrupt ending combined with the missing lyric will get the listener subconsciously frustrated enough to either play the song again, or continue singing the song against his will for a prolonged time after the song is complete.

Creating the feel of a crowd for familiarity is not just limited to the song itself. The visual elements of a song will also lend credence to the crowd mentality, and the viewer can feel comfortable joining the group. The thinking would be: "I can see that everyone else is doing it, so I should, as well." Pointing again to the Randy Newman example, the video constantly shows multiple people singing the "We love it!" chant at every instance except the final one, almost guilting the viewer into joining in.

Just having a crowd around can easily enhance a song that does not have a natural call-and-response. When Billy Ray Cyrus came out with "Achy Breaky Heart" in 1992, he was almost completely unknown. Very few people would come out to see him, let alone do the dance that accompanied the song. The record label changed all that by filming the video in front of a crowd of what appeared to be a few thousand people, many of whom did the line dance. This made Cyrus appear to be already huge, and an established phenomenon to which the rest of the world needed to catch up. This has been a tried-and-true marketing method for many years, and will only increase as access to videos gets easier and the need to establish the large communal fan base becomes greater.

All of the repetition techniques used to entice the listener to sing, and many of the techniques described in this book, are utilized to both gain awareness and usage from an active listener, or to engage a passive listener to become active with that particular song. Large numbers of people will rarely, if ever, look at music actively. This is why Adult Contemporary has consistently been one of the most listened to radio formats. The passive nature of the audience has made dollars harder to earn for such songs, as they often sold less than active songs. Subsequently, record companies have minimized their development dollars for artists of this style.

The changing nature of distribution and income streams will change all that.

11

CREATE MELLOW
BACKGROUND MUSIC

Over the years, background music has been called many things. In a positive spin, it has been called "Soft Pop," "Adult Contemporary," or "Adult Pop." In a negative slant, it has been called "Elevator Music" or "Dentist Office Music." The company that started the trend, Muzak, was once a very innovative and positive name. It has since devolved into a one-word joke for a sound that music fans and critics routinely deride as dull and boring.

The truth is large numbers of people actually like this music, preferring inoffensive, soothing songs with no distractions. Even if they do not want that music all the time, they do desire that mellow mood in many specific situations. This includes listening to music in an office while working, relaxing at home, and that proverbial visit to a doctor. The reason they like the music is because it is so passive. Done right, it never annoys, yet provides lilting familiar melodies. But it never engages the listener to become active.

MELLOW RADIO PLAY

This has made it a difficult business for record labels to profit in during the past decade. Radio stations that cater to these listeners use extensive research for every song they play, and songs usually have to be very familiar in order to make it onto a tightly controlled playlist. However, in order to create familiarity, record companies need that radio station airplay. This Catch-22 situation, along with the difficulty in selling this product, caused most labels to back away from signing such artists. Any songs that make it onto these formats come from artists such as Mariah Carey who really belong in another popular genre, but created a song mellow enough to qualify. By the time these songs got popular outside of the soft pop world, they had a mass appeal that made them safer for radio programmers to play. Recent artists that do play solely to this genre, such as Norah Jones and Josh Groban, got the radio play only after they were fortunate enough to either create a prolonged critical groundswell or obtain exposure from television. They also succeeded in selling big numbers because they had little competition.

Once an artist does get on these adult stations, the next hurdle is translating that airplay into actual sales. Once again, the passive nature of the songs creates a climate whereby the listener is seldom engaged enough to purchase the product. Additionally, the repetitive, familiar nature of these stations means the songs would be heard often. This is an additional disincentive for the listener to purchase the music, since the listener would feel the song was always on. The inability to drive revenue just hammers one more nail in the coffin, and record labels avoid developing these acts. Why bother spending the money if the chances for making it back are slim?

THE MELLOW PART
OF THE LONG TAIL

Part of the reason for this sea change has to do with the popular "Long Tail" theory. This theory is detailed in Chris Anderson's book, *The Long Tail: Why The Future Of Business Is Selling Less Of More.* It argues that the Internet, and its ability to store and have access to more titles than could ever be housed in a physical location, creates significant revenue opportunities for those titles on the margin. The theory holds weight, as usage and purchasing in recent years is up for artists long thought to be either dormant and/or marginal. Universal Music Group recently corroborated the theory with a test of titles that were long unavailable and were subsequently made available digitally without marketing. Nearly all of these titles generated enough sales to make it a profitable venture.

Long tail endorsers love to use this theory to prop up the newfound viability in critically acclaimed music on the fringe. Artists in these genres, such as Americana or Indie Rock, often have great difficulty convincing traditional gatekeepers of their relevance, and subsequently have trouble obtaining exposure. With the validity of the long tail theory, these artists now receive much more exposure than before, resulting in small, but substantial increases in their revenue. The downside is that these fringe acts will likely still remain on the fringe, and continue to have difficulty in achieving revenue levels that are feasible for a full-time career. These artists also tend to be skipped more than those of other genres, leading to lower streaming revenue. The audience that enjoys artists in fringe genres also consumes greater quantities of songs from multiple artists. This leads to lower repetitive play, which in turn makes familiarity and the dollars that come with it more difficult to achieve per exposure.

Often lost in this discussion are the styles of music that exist on the margins and offer greater growth potential within the long tail. Most mellow and background music actually falls into this category. Its limited placement on the radio and lower sales potential, not to mention the passive nature of the music, has made overall visibility of this genre's popularity hard to gauge. The number of new mellow artists signed to major labels in recent years has been small, which has also made this genre's popularity difficult to measure.

The most listened to radio station in the United States is WLTW, an Adult Contemporary station in New York City. The average listener spends nine hours a week listening to the station, as compared to averages of six hours for urban stations, 5 1/4 hours for rock stations, and five hours for pop stations. The numbers for Internet radio is similar. On AOL, three of the Top Five most listened to stations are mellow genres. On Yahoo! Music, the station "Lite Office Music" is often in the Top Five as well.

BACKGROUND LISTENING

The fact that a station called "Lite Office Music" attracts such a large audience shines a spotlight on online listening patterns. Most of the discussion on Internet music tends to focus on active audiences using the web to find, develop, and discover rock, urban, and pop talent. Those active people are not the ones spending the most time consuming legal online music. Many people at their offices are tethered to their computer for most of their eight-hour workday. They often work in relative isolation to others, and their jobs can be tedious, monotonous, and boring. But whereas offices used to have one centralized stereo that broadcast music, workers now listen to individual music streams on headphones through their computer or iPods without bothering anyone else. The stress often found in the workplace necessitates a calming presence, and softer music is a regular source that provides that.

This workplace usage is also the bigger audience, even if it is not usually the most prominent. According to Arbitron and Edison Media Research, the time slot with the highest online radio audience is Monday through Friday from 10 A.M. until 3 P.M., nearly double that of the next measured slot. Also, while teenagers and college kids are assumed to be the biggest users of Internet radio, the over thirty-five audience actually accounts for more than 60% of all online radio listening. This audience is quietly the true, non-hip driver of Internet music commerce.

As a natural extension, there is also significant usage in background listening situations outside of the workplace. One of the common ones is studying. Though the usage of lite music in this situation is less so than in the office (due to the younger demographic), there are still considerable numbers of young people who want to be soothed, and not agitated while studying. As more people link their computers to their main entertainment systems (either by iPod connections or wireless media routers), background music within the home will become more dominated by digital media play, as opposed to physical media play. As people play background music for cocktail parties, house cleaning, and reading the Sunday paper, more of these experiences will come through media that either directly or indirectly results from digital experiences.

Adding up all these regular usages, airplay numbers for songs in these genres are higher per capita. The need for familiarity within background music listening will also insure that these play events occur for a period of time much longer than other forms of pop music. This keeps play counts at high levels, with very little station switching or skipping, and a much higher time spent listening per session.

With airplay numbers reaching higher levels, they will begin to have a greater impact on record industry charts. These titles will then be far more prominent on charts, and make up a greater proportion of chart positions than in recent years. This will build the viability of the song in the marketplace, which will lead to even more airplay on existing outlets, and new airplay on new outlets. The cycle will continue for many weeks as these songs gain a stronger foothold within the chart.

The higher percentage of these titles on the chart will reignite the interest in background music as a format. This will inevitably lead to more choices in companies and individuals spreading this genre. Naturally, this leads to even more exposure and higher chart positioning. What has largely been a genre marginalized by the hype of new aggressive music forms will become a very visible market opportunity in a few short years.

HISTORY OF MELLOW POPULARITY SPIKES

This also follows historical precedence with other technologies. In its infancy in the late 1960s, FM radio was a wild frontier, now best remembered for the reckless DJs and stations that programmed counter-culture rock music with great abandon. Like the Internet's early days, these tastemakers championed eclectic new artists that began to take hold in the marketplace, and became the classic rock stars of today. The format was initially freeform. But it eventually came to be called AOR for Album Oriented Rock, because these DJs were never satisfied in playing only one single from an album. They would go deep into other songs, exposing their audience to the wide variety of music available. Legends such as the Grateful Dead, Jimi Hendrix, Frank Zappa, and Led Zeppelin got their start within this renegade use of new technology, and were considered musical underdogs.

After approximately ten years, as the medium matured into the late 1970s, the AOR train continued to run, but big business morphed up the alphabet as the "A" changed to an "M" for the most popular FM format. MOR stood for Middle Of the Road, and was everything the forward-thinking AOR programmers railed against. It morphed the old standards into a more contemporary, lite music sound, and it was boring and it was background. It was the Carpenters, Carly Simon, and Andy Gibb. And it was also enormously successful, bringing in huge audiences.

Yet most of the MOR audience did not adapt to it early or quickly. The cool college kids looking for the newest and latest bought into FM radio in the late 1960s, and it was only many years later that the adults followed en masse. This timeline nearly follows the rise of the Internet in recent years. Today, the public is culturally in the same place that the adult audience was in during the late 1970s. Now that mainstream listeners have adapted to high speed Internet and are comfortable with navigating, their voices will be heard with the large cume audiences they will deliver for this sound.

A fundamental difference between the late 1970s and today is the potential revenues for these songs. These artists were often a considerable financial gamble for a record label. Airplay did not always translate into sales. In most cases, the number of radio plays needed to sell a copy of an Adult Contemporary record is much higher than that of other formats. There is very little spark or impetus to drive someone into a record store toward a purchase. As opposed to hyper AOR DJs who blathered on excitedly about a particular artist's musical acumen, an MOR DJ had a soothing voice that blended into the background. In fact, it blended so neatly that oftentimes a listener might not even realize a person was speaking, let alone pay attention to what was being said. With all these factors, it is no surprise few people paid for this music.

In many cases, mellower songs also move at slower tempos than other facets of pop music. A lot of this has to do with the heart rate of the listener, who is often subconsciously seeking music to complement or counteract his mood. Perhaps the user is stressed and looking for music to soothe and relax his body, or bring his "boiling blood" down to a comfortable level. Playing background music at work allows the listener to remain calm and levelheaded as he accomplishes the stressful tasks at hand. In nearly every conceivable situation, the style and vibe that the audience demands will result in a slower tempo than often found in most popular music.

MELLOW PAYMENTS

This now leads to increased royalties and revenues. If the songs are slower, then they also have a tendency to be longer. If the song is longer, it will have an easier ability to earn a higher percentage of royalties per hour than other songs. It will also play longer, preventing other songs from being heard and exposed to the audience. This, in turn, will allow these songs to chart more easily and prevent other songs from either charting or earning money.

This is something that has been relatively standard for the genre. In the popular music era, 80% of #1 songs that have exceeded five minutes could easily be considered a part of background music. Making it even easier to secure full-length airplay and royalties of these long songs is the lack of responsiveness from this listener. Audiences of other popular music formats are very interactive and move very swiftly between songs. As a result, they are unlikely to hear significant portions of many songs, resulting in their difficulty in remembering them, which naturally affects the songs' income potential. In contrast, the background music audience tends to be passive throughout the experience, making them less likely to actually move between songs. Therefore, more songs are heard to their completion in this genre than any other. This results in new songs having a higher percentage of royalty generating plays, and a higher likelihood of being remembered by the listener.

All of these factors add up to significant revenue potential. As the audience shifts to digital transmissions, every single listen results in a royalty paid to a record company. The overall effect of the longer listening time, the ever-increasing cume, the repetitive airplay within the genre, the longer lengths of the songs, and the burgeoning visibility of this genre as a whole, highlights a climate that will likely foster the biggest growth in online royalties. Also, unlike pop songs, these titles hold their success longer, resulting in a greater time period for the artist to reap financial benefits. All this repetition results in significant familiarity, which increases the likelihood that it will be a viable catalog title in future years. With such a strong climate, a mellow song easily has much better odds of achieving financial viability in the long run than songs in other popular musical genres.

NON-MELLOW ARTISTS MELLOWING OUT

This will not only occur with artists who create music solely in this genre. If anything, select songs will be recorded by cool, credible artists who subtly morph into a mellower style, allowing for expansive potential airplay to this market. Since the digital world is largely a song-based economy, these artists can easily create songs for that audience with revenue-generating potential in mind. Previously, a listener might not have purchased a full-length record from such an artist, knowing he would like only the one mellow song. Now, that artist can make significant revenue from streaming and sales revenue of that sole track.

Having one mellow song is a tact that many metal acts took in the 1980s and early 1990s. Artists such as Motley Crue and Poison were renowned for their wild party antics and loud guitar music, with everything turned up to eleven. Yet their greatest successes occurred with mellow ballads that had little to do with the majority of the music they created. Nowhere was this more "extreme" than with the band Extreme. They included two acoustic songs on their metal record *Extreme II: Pornograffitti*, one of which was called "More Than Words." This song quickly became a huge hit, but also led many listeners to believe Extreme was a soft rock band. When these fans purchased the record and found that "More Than Words" was not representative of the band's sound, and the majority of the record was loud metal, many customers were extremely irate and returned the album. This song still remains popular on Adult Contemporary stations, and is reaping additional financial benefits now that significant royalties are generated with the song decoupled from the full-length album.

Artists will likely experiment as they look for the balancing act between keeping their audience base of "cool kids" while still reaping financial benefits of having a successful background song. This will be more about effective marketing than anything else. Still, the income that a highly successful background song can bring in will increase in attraction as other songs fail to bring in enough money. The more bands that do this successfully, the more other bands will want to participate. Then it will be "socially acceptable," even among the hippest of groups.

Background music's repetition will not be the only driver in creating familiarity. The songs themselves—and the ways people get those songs—will also help break certain artists in the future. The fact that the Internet can provide a response time unrivaled by other previous recorded media also marks a significant shift in song marketing for individual artists. Exploiting this at the song level will also create change that will result in higher awareness and revenues for artists. Once again, achieving this just requires a look back in pop music history.

12

COVER VERSIONS

OF HIT SONGS

Cover songs are among the easiest recordings an artist can produce, even though they can also be the most expensive. An artist's recording is owned and controlled by a particular owner (usually a record label), and any usage of that recording, in whole or in part, has to come with permissions from that owner. For popular songs, such permissions often carry hefty price tags. The actual song the artist records, however, can be utilized with a virtually guaranteed permission for a modest rate, which is firmly established. This essentially allows anyone to record any song he wants at any time.

This automatic granting of rights stems from the Copyright Act of 1976. In that act, the government stated that once a song is officially released as a recording, anyone could record an alternate version of that song without consent from the copyright owner, usually a publishing company. In exchange for this, an artist only needs to obtain the compulsory license and agree to pay a government determined standard rate. In 2006, that rate stood at 9.1 cents per use and has remained at that level since then. A recording artist can, and often gets, lower rates than this, but in general, as long as he agrees to pay the 9.1 cents every time the song gets sold, he can record and release the song.

With slimming profit margins from recorded music, paying that fee might appear too expensive. If the song-releasing environment grows to necessitate releasing more songs per year than the current schedules, artists will need to find more songs. If the artist is not a songwriter, he often pays songwriters more to use a song first, so cover versions are actually a cheaper alternative. If the artist is a songwriter, covers allow for a steady product release in times of creative drought. Releasing a good song regularly is now vital to a career, so song quality is crucial. The money spent on covers is actually a savings, as the artist knows original songs will not always have the same resonance with the public.

HISTORY OF COVERS

Cover songs in recent years have been largely looked upon as a novelty. In the 1990s and the beginning of this century, many labels put together tribute albums on which major stars paid homage to influential artists as wide ranging as KISS, Elton John, Duran Duran, the Pixies, and more. The albums usually experienced modest sales, and often these versions were forgotten within the covering artists' catalog. Mostly, they are known as rarities and curios among the die-hard fans. Only in isolated instances, such as the all-star *Moulin Rouge!* soundtrack cover of "Lady Marmalade," does a cover song actually transcend this stigma to become a significant song in its own right.

This outlook is actually in opposition to what the music buying public has traditionally desired. Most people care more about the song than who is doing the singing. Before recorded music, classical and popular music's fame centered on songs and composers instead of the artist. Multiple performers would usually deliver the songs that were most popular at the moment. As recorded music gained favor, this tradition continued with popular songs receiving treatment by multiple artists at the height of a song's popularity. While some songs achieved mass popularity via one version by one artist, it was common to see songs become successful with multiple versions released around the same time.

As music entered the rock era, cover versions continued to flourish on and off the pop charts. A popular trend in the early rock era grew out of racism and cultural polarization. R&B records were highly reactive in major cities, but some record stores refused to stock and sell releases by the black artists who recorded them. White artists such as Pat Boone re-recorded these songs, primarily for a white audience, and usually in a softer tone. Those versions achieved great pop and financial success, mostly because they were the only versions available in certain stores.

Jazz artists were also spreading the word of that era's talent by covering their compositions. With mass media still in its infancy and existing media focusing on the burgeoning rock scene, jazz musicians relied on multiple artists to popularize their work. John Coltrane and Thelonious Monk would have been less likely to become legendary figures were it not for the efforts of many artists at the time recording and playing their tunes.

In the 1960s, the industry began to sign singer-songwriters. This was due both to their rise in popularity and so the record labels could save some money. Rather than obtaining a mechanical license from Harry Fox and dealing with first-use negotiations, the labels found it easier and more affordable to keep it all self-contained within the artists themselves. Until this point, most artists were not expected to be both singer and songwriter. The economic realities--coupled with the burgeoning creativity of Baby Boomers entering adulthood--produced this new outlook. While the industry was transitioning to this model, numerous artists found success by covering the singer-songwriter stars of the era, such as Bob Dylan and the Beatles.

In the 1970s, cover versions began to lose favor. As the singer-songwriter growth coincided with the expansion of the album format, artists had little incentive to cover other songs. The death knell sounded in the late 1970s when the most popular cover songs were disco dance versions of songs from a variety of eras. Music fans had little respect for what was seen as cocaine-fueled, sacrilegious takes on important musical works.

THE COPYRIGHT ACT AND CONTROLLED COMPOSITION

The higher statutory payments mandated by the Copyright Act of 1976 all but sealed the deal for cover versions. Record labels, in signing singer-songwriters, created a "controlled composition" clause in their contracts. This meant that since the artist also controlled the songs being recorded, and since these usages were debuting on the artist's record, the labels could set a cap on the number of songs for which they would pay. Further keeping costs under control, the labels also began to only pay 3/4 of the rate set by the government. This quickly became industry standard, and few artists were able to excise it from their contracts.

This scenario quickly created a situation that severely discouraged an artist to record a cover song. Presume that an artist's contract allowed for ten songs at the 3/4 rate per album. At the current rate, this would create a pool of 68 1/4 cents per album. Say an artist wished to make a twelve-song album, of which four of the songs were covers and eight were originals. Unless he negotiated otherwise, the artist would have to pay the full rate on the four songs, which would amount to 36.4 cents. This would then leave just under thirty-two cents for the singer-songwriter's eight songs, which is just under four cents a song, or less than half of what the government mandates should be paid for the same song. It is clearly not in the artist's best interest to include covers on his albums.

With the image of the cover song tarnished by cheap disco versions and financial incentives to record these songs now diminished, it is not surprising that covers became a rare occurrence. This also happened at a time when the album was more important than the song. With singles disappearing from the marketplace in the 1990s, the attitude shifted further away from the need for cover songs.

Record labels also allowed their artists more time in between albums to record the right hit songs, thus not demanding releases on a quick schedule. This virtually eliminated the need for many artists to solicit cover songs. Exceptions occurred when record labels, after attempting to find a hit single for an artist, resorted to finding a suitable cover in order to gain some return on their investment. Rock bands such as Alien Ant Farm and Orgy were generally derided in serious music circles for their respective Michael Jackson and New Order covers, and failed to have any significant hits outside of that one song.

FAMILIARITY IN A DIGITAL ERA

The new digital era of music consumption is rapidly changing the attitude of cover versions. The increasing demands of artists and songwriters—coupled with new economic realities forced upon every aspect of the business—will practically force cover versions to become a regular part of many artists' release schedule. It is one of those situations where multiple forces begin to coincide at the same point to move the marketplace in that direction, whether it wants to or not.

The increasingly distracted audience is easily the biggest reason to go in this direction. The distractions that music listeners experience for all forms of entertainment constantly make it hard for them to retain familiarity on any song. As a result, many artists will have two options: Figure out a way to ensnare a listener with something familiar, or take advantage of their confusion by having them inadvertently go to the cover over the original version.

The confusion over ownership of the song may not be apparent to hardcore music fans, but it is a reality to average music buyers. Most people have little commitment to the artist who actually sings a song. They may like a couple of particular artists, but in general they like songs and could not care less who sings them. As they explore these songs, they will encounter these alternate cover versions. If the version is good, the usual lack of time with multiple distractions will give that song a high likelihood of generating that additional revenue.

When the listener is confronted with a song, melody, lyric or chord progression that strikes him as instantly familiar, the listener will have a much higher likelihood of sticking through the entire song. He may do so just because of the familiarity, or out of curiosity as to how the artist will add something new. Either way, it has a positive impact in creating awareness for the artist, and increases the likelihood that the listener will test out other songs by that same artist.

In recent years, this was mostly achieved via music samples, which created an entirely new song out of familiar melodies and, additionally, utilized the actual recording of the hit song. This often proved to be an expensive proposition, as the artist had to pay for both the songwriter and the performer of the sample. When those are one and the same, the cost may be reasonable. When they are not, the price can be exceptionally high. For example, Rihanna's hit, "SOS," sampled the song "Tainted Love." The songwriter was Ed Cobb, whose publisher had to be paid for the new usage. The artist was Soft Cell, whose only substantial hit was the sample being utilized. Since Soft Cell did not write "Tainted Love," they made far less money on the song than if they had. With the sample in high demand, Soft Cell was likely able to command a premium royalty for use of this particular sample. This enabled the duo to generate more money, but made the profit margins for Rihanna and her label, Island Def Jam, much lower.

If the familiarity angle is what the artist wants, the desired effect can be achieved much cheaper by creating a cover. Studio wizardry can also create similar sounds to the original version without having to resort to sampling. As computer software homogenizes the many sounds, notes, and beats created for a song, it can also generate a potential "soundalike" of just about any artist. This was heretofore stigmatized, but is quickly becoming acceptable in music circles.

PRODUCERS AND MIX TAPES

In many instances, it may not just be the artist starting from scratch. Producers will also create cover versions of their own songs, albeit with slightly different melodies and lyrics. As many current hits remain beat-driven, producers will find it very tempting to take a successful rhythm they created for artist A, and then have artist B come by the next day to do a different version. As labels attempt to squeeze producers to accept lower fees for their songs, relinquishing some exclusivity on beats will be a likely tradeoff. With that, producers will probably make the same money for the track they have made in previous years, but it will be spread out over several artists.

This is hardly a new concept, as it largely stems from the cost saving measures that Jamaican producers have used for years. In the 1970s, when modern recording technology reached the island, producers began to use backing tracks over and over by having different singers provide unique lyrics to the rhythms. Occasionally, the producers would add reverb and other effects to the same backing tracks to subtly distinguish one version from another. As computerized dancehall beats infiltrated the culture, the practice only increased. By doing this, producers could maximize the profits they would receive from a track and, simultaneously, make it more familiar by having more artists promoting the track as part of their discography.

In the U.S., this has been occurring within hip-hop circles for a long time, but mostly via the underground mix tape circuit. Artists and/or DJs take the instrumental tracks of hit songs and add an entirely new rap. This track is mixed in with other legitimate and illegitimate versions to create a consistent theme. These versions are well liked, as they often project rawness not found in studio recordings, and are created quickly and cheaply. They also add credibility to the artist on the streets with a combination of immediate, honest lyrics reflecting current cultural events along with the underlying disregard of the original copyright.

Artists, publishers, and record labels have been mostly overlooking this practice, as the community accepts it with a wink and a nod. As revenue streams tighten up, and people realize the potential profit margins should these songs be legitimately released, they will start becoming a much larger part of an official catalog. No one will be able to ignore the revenue and promotional potential of such pairings, and all parties will begin to exploit this consumer demand in a legitimate fashion. The arrest in early 2007 of DJ Drama, one of the more successful DJs in the business, is seen as a first step toward bringing this practice into the industry mainstream. His operation sold tens of thousands of mix CDs monthly, and his arrest underscores the vast income this end of the business may generate.

The repetition of rhythms has already been attempted legitimately to some degree, with mixed degrees of success. In 2003, the Diwali rhythm, which is essentially a sample, was used in hits by Sean Paul ("Get Busy"), Lumidee ("Never Leave You"), and Missy Elliott ("Pass That Dutch"). The collective body of songs likely generated substantial revenues for the Diwali producer, Steve "Lenky" Marsden. Producers will now take the lessons learned from this and begin to actively apply them for a more profitable approach to music making.

The need to increase an artist's recorded output will also be a major impetus to record cover versions. Most artists will not be prolific enough to generate the number of original tunes needed to meet what is certain to be a demanding schedule. Between recording and releasing more songs per year, the demands of touring and promotion, and the expected additional pull of press and publicity as multiple online outlets grow in importance, most artists will simply not have enough time to create quality original music. Many of them will be offered new songs from both new and established songwriters. However, many artists will gravitate to a much easier solution: Go to what you know.

SEARCH PATTERNS

The demands will be greater on new artists who need to make a mark quickly in an increasingly competitive environment. The company that has dealt with a high volume of new artists in this new digital age is CDBaby. This business was the first to offer every independent artist the ways and means to feature and distribute his CDs via the Internet. Some artists sell only a couple of copies, while others have gone on to sell tens of thousands, making a much larger profit in the process. As the company moved into the digital age selling individual downloads, founder Derek Sivers noticed that certain unknown artists were selling at higher rates than anticipated. He quickly identified the common trend—cover songs.

As people search for a song on popular retail destinations such as iTunes and eMusic, they often find that the original version has not yet been cleared for digital sales, but has been re-recorded by an enterprising independent artist. Although the new version will not sell to the degree that the original version would, whether it is available or not, there is a noticeable lift in sales of this newly recorded version. Many people, who like this new version, go on to purchase more material from the artist discovery. In March 2008, when "American Idol" contestant Jason Castro sang the song "Hallelujah," the Jeff Buckley cover that he imitated immediately jumped to #1 on the digital sales chart and increased over 7,000% in sales in one week. In the same week, Leonard Cohen's original version also jumped up nearly 600%, and a Michael McDonald version released at the same time managed to sell over 500 copies, as well. In the summer of 2008, Kid Rock had a massive hit with "All Summer Long," but his label refused to sell it as an a-la-carte download. When people searched for the song on iTunes, they were unable to find the original version, but did find a version by "The Rock Heroes." Subsequently, that version sold hundreds of thousands of copies, as consumers were distracted in not realizing it was not the original. Other versions by artists like "Hit Masters" and "Starlite Singers" also sold well.

"WHAT HURTS THE MOST"

The importance of releasing covers becomes apparent at the occasional moment when a record label withholds a popular title from digital sales in the hopes of artificially creating noise the first week it is available. If there is an alternate version available, that song can reap the reward. In 2006, the popular country group Rascal Flatts decided that the first single from their new album was going to be a cover of a Mark Wills song, "What Hurts the Most." In order to avoid diminishing first-week album sales figures, the label held back the release of the digital single so consumers could not purchase it.

At this point, the cover version theory went into effect. The original Mark Wills version, recorded three years earlier, was quietly sitting on digital shelves, collecting proverbial cyberdust. It had barely moved since its release, rarely selling more than ten downloads a week. When the song took off, people immediately rushed to iTunes to purchase the track. The only song they could find was the Mark Wills version. Despite the fact that Rascal Flatts is one of the biggest groups in country music, with instant name recognition, thousands of people still thought the Mark Wills song was what they were looking for, and purchased the track.

Finally, a couple of weeks before the album was released, Rascal Flatts' record label, Lyric Street, released the song digitally. Instead of the expected spike with consumers finding the correct version, the Mark Wills rendition outsold the hit version in its first week. In fact, it continued to outsell the hit for four weeks, until the Rascal Flatts album was released. At the end of the run, Mark Wills sold about 90,000 downloads, almost exclusively from people looking for the other hit version. It still sells between fifty and one hundred downloads a week, as much as ten times the sales before this occurred.

Another trick that ended up prolonging the shelf life of the Mark Wills version was that search indexes order results by popularity. With the Rascal Flatts version unavailable, computer algorithms perceived the Mark Wills version as being more popular. This remained in effect for several weeks after the hit version was released. When consumers were finally able to compare both versions, they would see the Mark Wills rendition as being more popular, even though it actually was not. This ranking just led to more sales, and allowed more revenues to be generated for Wills.

INCREASED PRODUCT OUTPUT AND SPEED

Exploiting cover versions to satiate the demands of a hectic recording schedule is nothing new, particularly with burgeoning artists. Once again, this hearkens back to the 1950s and 1960s, when most artists did not have enough original material to support an exploding career. No act better exemplifies this than the Beatles, whose first few albums contained covers such as "Roll Over Beethoven," "Please Mr. Postman," and "Rock & Roll Music." Even though John Lennon and Paul McCartney would become the greatest and most prolific songwriters of the rock era, their early career was not made entirely of original material.

The speed in which songs can be created and released is another change in the music climate that will cause cover versions to flourish. Up until a few years ago, the hurdles an artist had to jump over to get a song released, even in the best of circumstances, were daunting. With direct digital distribution and cheaper production, artists can now be more reactive, specifically when it comes to covering current hit songs.

Prior to the new millennia, an artist who wished to record a cover of a potential new hit would be whacked with a process that was cumbersome enough to discourage someone from even trying. Initial distribution methods were often slow and restrictive, allowing days or weeks before an artist would actually discover the song. Then, an artist had to book time in a recording studio, which was subject to the scheduling of that studio. Optimistically, the artist might be able to record the song in a day or two at considerable expense. They would then need to ship the song to a record company who would need significant time to manufacture the song, either as a single or as part of a full-length release. They would also need several weeks of solicitation to retail to get a store to agree to stock the cover version. By the time it made it into a store to generate revenues, the original song would likely no longer be a hit. This is another reason why dance songs were more likely to be covers, as the independent labels that released them were more attuned to the streets and therefore quicker to reduce this timeline. Realistically, on a major label, this whole process would take eight to twelve weeks.

The new millennium offers a much different picture, allowing a quick, reactive approach to getting a cover song out into the marketplace. An artist can hear the song on the day of release, and since the Internet makes it easy to become aware of that song immediately, the artist can then go into his home recording studio and make his own version at minimal cost. This song can then be uploaded onto the net and into major online retailers and promotional outlets with quick speed. Even when dealing with major label paperwork, this process would likely take one to two weeks. The nimble independent labels can potentially have it up in one *day* on their own controlled sites, and in about a week on the big digital retailers.

This nimbleness allows artists to test and build more catalog than they ever have before. Even if the song were poorly received, the perception would likely be one of experimentation. The speed in which the song can be released would also likely mean that a marketing plan would be a secondary thought, further minimizing potential long-term damage to the artist should the cover version not be high quality. If, in fact, the cover version *is* received positively, the label can quickly enact a marketing plan to capitalize on this song's newfound popularity. It can also use it to exploit other songs in the artist's discography.

Artists who do not want to sacrifice a portion of publishing revenue, or who feel that cover versions negatively affect an artist's integrity, can always record a song with the same title as a popular song. Consumer confusion will result in some people accidentally discovering the similarly titled song, just because it shows up in a search listing.

As cover versions become more prominent, many consumers will also be interested in discovering all the interpretations of their favorite song. The song, not the artist, becomes the art. Much like certain conductors adapting classical works, the audience is interested to see what differences and nuances another artist might bring to a particular work. While this bumps up the airplay of all cover versions, it also increases the likelihood that other songs with the same title will also experience significant and unexploited exposure. Gnarls Barkley's 2006 hit, "Crazy," took on a new life after covers were quickly spread by other artists such as the Kooks, Nelly Furtado, Ray LaMontagne, Cat Power, and the Zutons. Undoubtedly, the song's success led new fans to discover classic songs with the same title, such as Patsy Cline's version of the Willie Nelson standard.

The act of exploiting the cover is one of bringing substantial familiarity to the listener. It does not take long for him to become more engaged in the song if it is done well. The experience feels comfortable, and is therefore easily embraced. Naturally, there are many other techniques that also make the listener feel more comfortable with a song. As individual song plays start to mean real dollars to the artist, comfort, as it relates to increased airplay, will grow as a factor. As we shall see, most people find comfort in songs that respond to the natural rhythms of their day.

13

THE WALKING BEAT

One of the most indelible opening segments in movie history perfectly marries music and visuals to set the tone for the main character and the theme of the film. This impact is so strong that anyone who sees the movie can likely conjure up the image just at the mere mention of it. It introduces the protagonist without even showing his full body, but his cocksure swagger says it all.

"STAYIN' ALIVE"

The film is *Saturday Night Fever.* John Travolta is shown during the opening credits walking down a Brooklyn sidewalk, with the emphasis on his steps. He walks in time with the Bee Gees' "Stayin' Alive" as if he and the song are one. The film and the song became permanently linked to disco and, via this extremely strong opening sequence, "Stayin' Alive" became arguably the biggest disco song ever released.

The interesting anomaly is that "Stayin' Alive" is not typical of most disco songs. Disco was the offspring of several factors that collided with each other in the early to mid-1970s. As with other forms of music, the technology of nightclub music changed dramatically during that time. Public address systems were developed that amplified pre-recorded music to a level unheard prior to this era. In 1971, a company led by Rudy Bozak introduced a mixer that allowed high-quality sound tweaking of multiple sound sources. In 1977, the same year *Saturday Night Fever* was released, an affordable mixer with the first cross-fader suddenly made DJ mixing a viable option for many smaller clubs and mobile DJs. Even developments in lighting and other effects heavily impacted this rise, including the smoke machine in the mid-1970s.

Another factor that had a huge impact in the creation of the music was not technological, but sociological. Cocaine became widely available in nightclubs that played disco music. What had been relegated to the margins of society quickly became in vogue for hip city dwellers, who moved from recreational use of marijuana and LSD in college in the 1960s to recreational use of pills and cocaine in the workforce in the 1970s. Much as rock music of the late 1960s was influenced and enhanced by pot smoking, people were looking for a music experience that enhanced their enjoyment of being high on cocaine.

Some musicians, who had previously smoked large amounts of pot in creating those new forms of rock music in the 1960s, were now snorting large amounts of cocaine in crafting disco. To obtain that enhancement of the cocaine high, musicians stepped up the tempos for dance music, which increased along with the listener's heart rate. The songs sped along at a consistently higher speed, and many of them nearly replicated the increased heart rate that accompanied cocaine use. The dancer felt the euphoria and became one with the music's synchronous tempos.

Which is what makes "Stayin' Alive" both an anomaly, and yet completely logical in its placement as the most popular disco song. This tune was not born from the clubs, but instead succeeded on radio. The tempo of a person walking is much slower than the cocaine heart rhythms in the club. In fact, while "Stayin' Alive" is indelibly linked to this disco film, the song is not used in any of the dancing scenes, either in or outside of the disco. The trademark Travolta dance move actually accompanied the song, "You Should Be Dancing," which had a much faster tempo.

The truth is that the nation was not high on cocaine at the time, and neither were the Bee Gees. Now, as then, drug use was concentrated to a minority. While some disco songs infiltrated the pop charts, many did not, because the rhythms were not comforting to most listeners. "Stayin' Alive" made disco more accessible by slowing down the rhythm to that walking pace. The original intention of the song was to match the footsteps of John Travolta, not to establish itself as the disco anthem for the ages. The tune became a major hit because it was a disco song with a beat that responded to the natural rhythms of most people.

When one thinks about the success of mellow music, as discussed in Chapter Eleven, one sees many songs falling in the seventy to eighty-five beats-per-minute range. This generally approximates the rate of an adult heart at rest. The walking tempo of approximately 105 beats per minute also closely syncs with the heart rate of most adults who are engaged in fairly active walking. By placing songs within this rhythm, the artist could have a higher chance of integrating that song into people's lives. In the case of "Stayin' Alive," most people actually do not have a significantly increased heart rate during dancing, so the song fits nicely into the rhythms they are most comfortable with during that activity.

The connection between "Stayin' Alive" and a natural heart rate was actually noted by doctors in late 2008. In a small study, Dr. David Matlock of the University of Illinois College of Medicine at Peoria found that doctors and students could perform chest compressions during CPR more effectively when done to the beat of "Stayin' Alive." The 103 beats per minute, coupled with the widespread familiarity of the song, are now causing the track to enter into the lexicon as a barometer for proper CPR implementation. The relation between the song and a natural heart rhythm could not be made any clearer.

The demand for songs with a walking tempo took a dramatic turn in the early 1980s through new technologies that made music portable. The introduction of the Sony Walkman in 1979 truly revolutionized music consumption. For the first time, a listener could take his own personal music selection with him into nearly any plausible situation. He could listen to his own music privately in a public place without having to hear other music or noise that surrounded him, and he could easily bring music with him when he traveled or worked. An image most people associate with the Walkman is of a jogger who could, for the first time, listen to music while he exercised. This added exercise enhancement no doubt contributed to the sudden rise in jogging during the same time. However, the biggest usage likely came from just plain everyday walking, as implied by the name of the device.

The one place that nobody had been able to consistently listen to music was in his routine daily travels. Unless you were in a car, the act of listening to music in between the events of your day was not physically possible. The Walkman enabled listening during these moments. For the first time, having music that comforted the listener as he walked seemingly became a necessity. The result was a significant uptake in songs with this tempo, though it is uncertain that hit music producers utilized the tempo specifically for this purpose.

As the 1990s signified a change from tapes to compact discs, a switch also occurred within portable music players. This switch did not go as smoothly for the average everyday walker, since the new portable CD players were bulkier than their cassette counterparts. While these players were useful for listening to music wherever you want, this mostly meant portability for the music while the listener was in a stationary position. When the devices were used in motion, they often jiggled and skipped, making total uninterrupted music listening a rarity. Their unwieldy size also often required the device to be placed elsewhere instead of a pocket, or clipped to a belt or pants.

This subconsciously may have led to a reduction in songs created with a walking tempo. At the same time, rock music tended to slow down as some rock musicians created their music on drugs that reduced their heart rates. Listeners also slowed down, as personified by the slacker stereotype, and therefore placed themselves in more situations in which their heart rate was at a slower, resting pace. Dance music, however, found faster rhythms as new drugs such as Ecstasy came in vogue, which ramped up heart rates faster than cocaine. While some songs did maintain the walking tempo, its usage was not as prevalent as in prior decades.

Today, the portability of music has returned with a vengeance. The iPod and all other portable digital music players have shrunk to sizes previously unforeseen in technology. The iPod shuffle is so compact it can comfortably be worn as a necklace. Many cheap flash-based players are easily worn on armbands. The iPod Nano is thin enough to be placed in a pocket. Other devices such as phones, watches, and even sunglasses are also now capable of holding songs, providing music portability to even larger portions of the population.

In 2006, emphasizing the connection between portable players, exercise, and the motion of the person using the device, Apple and Nike partnered to create a shoe that communicated with the iPod. The device would monitor a person's progress as he ran, and a voice coach would apprise him of his progress. The companies also commissioned artists to customize music that coordinated with a forty five minute workout routine. Fitness experts then put together playlists of songs that would help the user raise or lower his heart rate as appropriate. While a coach did not really offer instructions to "speed up" or "cool down," the tempo of the music dictated that, as people naturally attempted to move with the beat. The devices that manufactures will make in coming years will only enhance these types of relationships with consumers.

While certainly a portion of the audience will use these devices for high-intensity workouts, other activities will not make nearly the same impact on music usage. Individuals will not likely listen to an iPod while dancing in a group. The more probable scenario might be music played from an iPod at a party. From a royalty perspective, this would create one play listened to by multiple people. These plays will likely occur less often than individual plays heard over a user's headphones. This, in turn, will lead to less revenue, as these types of songs are purchased less often, since not everyone at the party needs to own them. In a subscription environment, these songs will generate fewer plays, as one play heard by forty people generates one payment, versus forty plays heard by forty people generating forty payments.

Most portable digital usage will occur during relatively calm periods of the listener's day. As discussed, users have become more accustomed to listening to the devices in hours of the day that previously had no music. The ease of carrying the device wherever you go means listening is possible while walking from one destination to the next, waiting in line, or just standing idly by. Nearly all of these quiet, passive usages will occur at points where the listener's heart rate is relaxed. The listener, by filling in these formerly silent periods of his days, will not be looking for music that would raise his heart rate. In fact, he will instinctively gravitate to music that matches his rhythms at the moment.

Even at points where there is little movement, listening will occur more often during a slightly active heart rate than relaxed slower periods. When a listener first wakes up in the morning, he is highly unlikely to go through the motions of getting a device, inserting headphones, and groggily selecting the right music. He may listen to the device prior to sleeping, but that period is limited, and occurs only once during the day. Most uses occur while the listener is fully alert, and likely doing other activities—reading, surfing the internet, playing games, or just combating boredom. In all instances, even with a more relaxed heart rate, the listener is awake.

The latest devices have much larger storage capacities, but that means the listener must devote more time to fill them. Previous portable devices required physically changing the music in order for the listener to have diversity. Having all the music one needs available at any given moment is helpful, but people still crave efficiency. Even with capacities that the average listener cannot fill, many users are including songs on their devices that only have a high likelihood of being played. With people naturally listening to more songs with a relaxed, walking tempo, the tendency will be to load the devices with these types of songs.

Most devices keep track of the person's listening habits. With one click, a user can listen to the songs he selects most often. This data does not come from perception, as previously required when one listened to music on physical media. This comes from actual tracking of the listener's actions. Most people perceive their listening habits to be far different from what they actually are. As they subconsciously listen to more songs at walking tempos, these songs will show up as the most played. This, in turn, will produce even more listens that perpetuate their place as a natural part of the listener's musical diet.

A higher inclination for these listening experiences will inevitably lead to bigger revenues for songs that play into this scenario. In subscription models, these songs will subtly receive more airplay, and therefore more revenues. In a purchasing scenario, these songs are more likely to be discussed by buyers. Eventually, these songs gain a slight competitive edge in charting, as the two forces will combine for more momentum on industry charts.

With all these listening events, the user will have a higher likelihood of discussing and/or singing these songs to friends and family. If he talks about it more, he is more likely to share the song. This immediately brings images of kids stealing music with wanton abandon. While this does occur, the best thing that could happen to a song is to have someone desire to share it. Even with theft, more sharing will, in fact, lead to more revenues. Sharing, however, just seems to happen, and the song's creators have little control over it. But here is an interesting idea to ponder: What would happen if songs were written with the explicit intent of sharing them?

14

CREATE THE NEED

TO SHARE SONGS

Most industry watchers consider file sharing the worst thing to happen to the music industry. They certainly are correct about the damage it does. The ease with which people steal music has made it very difficult to continue to grow the recorded music business. Sales are lost, and many in the industry cannot get remunerated for these illegal transactions.

On the other hand, most music fans consider file trading to be the *best* thing to happen to the music industry. They also are correct. People have never been more excited about music. The ability to hear songs before purchasing them allows users to make more educated decisions in insuring value received. It also allows access to obscure titles that were rarely available in local record stores.

How can both sides of this debate be correct? It is like a pendulum swinging side to side. The opposing sides are the industry and the consumers that it serves. By maintaining control of all the systems in which music is heard and sold, the record industry had the pendulum on its side for many years. Now with the Internet and file trading, the pendulum has swung to the consumers, and with a significant advantage. In fact, the excessive file trading has meant the swing is likely too far on the consumer side. In many ways, that correction might have been expected from decades of the pendulum lingering too long on the industry side. How did the pendulum swing so drastically?

MAP

Throughout much of the 1990s, the industry engaged in price fixing that kept the cost of music artificially high, and profits higher. While many people point to the rise in Napster as the beginning of the labels' decline, the seeds of the decline were sown several years before that. Around 1994, big box retailers began drastically undercutting wholesale prices of music in order to drive consumers into their stores for other purchases. The resulting price war supposedly led to several chains declaring bankruptcy, and many independent record stores closing their doors.

In 1995, in order to keep prices high, labels instituted a policy called MAP, which stood for Minimum Advertised Price. Under this agreement, labels spent marketing dollars with a particular record store for a release, as long as the record sold for a minimum price set by the label. If the store sold the CD for a lower price, the label would cut off all advertising dollars to that retailer. For the music retail eco-system, this made sense. It allowed the chains and smaller stores to have a more level playing field, so they would not lose business to big box retailers. It also kept label profits up. Not only did price wars with big box retailers end when MAP was implemented, but wholesale prices of CDs also dramatically increased soon after.

However, this quickly raised the concerns of many state attorney generals, as well as the Federal Trade Commission (FTC). Over the course of the next four years, they discovered one major problem: The labels basically colluded to create this policy. In a free market economy, the FTC held, a store should have the ability to charge any price it wants, even if that price is a loss. Also, lawyers argued, major labels could not conspire with each other to act in unison to insure compliancy for nearly 85% of the business. The case was strong, and the FTC decision was decisive: MAP was illegal.

The impact was already being felt prior to the decision. Feeling their backs against the wall, the labels began easing up on the policies in 1999. After the 2000 decision, mass merchants earnestly began selling the top releases below cost to drive people into the stores. The chain stores that charged the highest prices felt the pinch fastest, and sales started declining precipitously, just prior to the downturn of the industry as a whole. The prediction music industry analysts made came true over the ensuing years.

Napster's rise in 2000 became the scapegoat for the industry's problems. The industry painted a picture that showed that sales took a perilous decline due to rampant file trading. In other words, money was lost due to people stealing music. Music fans, however, took the opposite position. They pointed out that overall sales were never *higher* than when Napster was blooming in 2000. The labels' actions to shut down the service meant music discovery took a precipitous decline, and therefore people stopped buying those records.

In truth, both arguments had some factual basis, but masked the real damage of the government ban of MAP. The industry fears that created the policy in the first place were based mostly in reality. People wanted a bargain and did not want music prices to be too high. But along the way, other factors aided this decline. Napster's presence did bring down the value of music. By having it available free, regardless of whether users had access or not, the perception quickly took hold that list prices of eighteen to twenty dollars per CD were too high.

OTHER FACTORS FOR DECLINING CD SALES

Simultaneously, film companies found heavy consumer demand for DVDs. The DVDs looked like CDs, except they contained entire movies in high quality. The cost of a DVD on sale was nearly on par with the list price of a top-level CD. From the consumer perspective, why would sixty minutes of music cost the same as a two-hour movie, especially since the movie had better sound and additional features? This was hard to fathom, since the movie cost tens of millions to make, and the album far less. Even if the music had high desirability, it was difficult for consumers to find justification for such high prices.

Unfortunately, for retailers big and small, this all occurred during a real estate boom. While many people focus on the steep rise in housing prices during these years, the boom also hit retail locations. As the economy soared, rents in indoor and strip malls rose quickly. Retailers had to reconfigure budgets in the face of rising rents, when, coincidentally, music revenues declined due to increased competition from big box retail's lower pricing strategy.

These retailers had only a few choices. One was to expand their product line to include more high-margin items to keep up revenues. These sold briskly and helped stem the bleeding. But in order to accommodate DVDs, CD-Rs, and various novelty items, music shelf space had to be given up. This meant, over time, that fewer CDs could be sold, which resulted in a significant decline in those same CD sales. The other choice was to close the store. Many retailers also ended up choosing that route starting in 2000. That once unimaginable turn of events culminated with the close of the Tower Records chain in late 2006.

The net result is that the biggest culprit in declining sales in the 2000s was not file trading, but closed stores. If there are fewer stores, there are fewer opportunities to purchase records. The music industry likes to think that buying music is something that every person wants to do. The reality is that only a small subset actually cares about permanent music ownership. For most people, music is a pleasant diversion that does not need to be constantly fed by purchases. When they go to a mall and do not see a record store, they do not think about traveling to another destination so they can purchase the music they desire. Instead, most people purchase something else entirely, and the missed sale becomes a lost opportunity.

The decline, then, is complex and multi-layered. But nothing gets the blame like file trading. The industry was quick to assign heavily inflated figures of what piracy costs the industry. While the losses are real, there are many other factors to take into account. One is that a significant number of the thefts are committed by people who would not have purchased the music in the first place. Most people could never afford all of the music they wish to own. The costs are just too great. It does not make these actions ethically correct, but to assume that the theft came at the expense of a purchase is also presumptuous.

To see how true this argument is, one has only to look at catalog sales of classic artists over the last decade or so. The most in-demand songs within P2P systems are often classic artists, whose music has been out for decades. Millions own this music already, making it easy to find and steal. The conventional wisdom is that these artists would experience the largest negative sales impact. In truth, the opposite occurred. Pink Floyd's *Dark Side of the Moon,* long considered the most consistent catalog title, sold over half a million copies per year in three of the five years during the industry's "decline" of 2001 to 2006. From 1996 to 2000, this release sold 2.6 million copies. From 2001 to 2005, it sold 2.5 million copies. Statistically, this is even more remarkable considering the overall declines in sales from 2001 to 2005. Taken as a percentage of overall sales, it could be said that sales of *Dark Side of the Moon* actually *increased* at a time they should have been declining.

Numerous similar examples abound throughout the 2000s. If the artist's quality stayed high, and other market factors kept the artist in the public consciousness, then these records had a high likelihood of consistent sales. The ironic thing is that file trading of these very same records was also high during this time. It would seem counterintuitive that sales would remain high if people were stealing in such large numbers. But that is exactly what did occur. In fact, over all genres and all music new or old, the one consistent factor is that the top-selling titles are usually the top-swapped titles. In other words, the more demand there is to receive free content, the more likely it is to actually generate revenue.

There have been exceptions to this rule, but those titles generally came down to an issue of perceived quality. Some songs are stolen and also bought in large numbers because they are considered so good that masses of people have to own them. Other songs are stolen because the perception is that they are not worth the purchase price. Since the quality is assumed to be inferior, and the long-term ownership potential is minimal, sales are low, as the price is not commensurate to the quality. One thing is for certain: If a song is not traded heavily, it is unlikely to become a hit. Extensive file trading is now a fact of life for a hit song.

WORD OF MOUTH

The distinct advantage here is that when a hit song has the quality desired by the audience, the word (and the song) quickly spreads. People talk about these songs rapidly and easily. The more a song is talked about, the more likely it will generate revenue. This does not have to be the purchase of the track. It can come from watching a video on-demand on YouTube, listening to the song legally on-demand, making mobile purchases such as ringtones or master tones, or creating the necessary excitement that leads to licensing opportunities. It will also lead to repeat usages, as the consistent, increased chatter will remind listeners of the music. This will increase the likelihood of the listener experiencing the song a second time, further cementing the song in his brain.

This chatter is all-important, and can now take place through a variety of forms. Physical, one-to-one conversations are an obvious method. Cell phones have also given rise to more direct individual communications. It used to be that people could converse only when they were either face-to-face, or on a "land line" telephone with its limited mobility. This meant that several hours of a person's waking day were virtually unavailable for social conversation with specific people. Now those doors are wide open, and people can have those conversations at any moment, with very few limits, either verbally or through text messaging.

Of course, pay phones were also available at those times when one was mobile. However, pay phones were not an effective communication tool for the dissemination of musical knowledge. It is doubtful that someone would run to a cell phone and plunk in a quarter just to tell his friend he heard an amazing new song. Nor would most people carry enough change with them for five minutes on a pay phone, let alone a long-distance call. With cell phones, music fans are very likely to call a friend just to tell him about that amazing song, and the friend finds it socially acceptable to receive such calls with regularity. Costs are also cheap enough that there are more frequent long conversations between friends, which increase the possibility that music will come up as a topic.

If the information is short enough, or the communicator is in a situation that is not conducive to an audible conversation, text messaging is now an acceptable way to "talk." When that same person hears a song he wants to share with a friend, he can just text that information. Not only does this communication spread information quickly, but it also creates a semi-permanent record of the title, making this information easily accessible for the receiver when he wishes to hear the music.

If the person is tethered to a computer, email and instant messaging also become incredible tools, both for information dissemination and potential piracy. Accurate figures are hard to come by, but many industry experts believe that piracy of music through files sent via email or Instant Messenger are far more pervasive than the P2P sites most people associate with illicit activity. The ease at which music can be forwarded and spread allows the positive (or negative) word to spread with astounding speed and credibility. Although most associate this communication flow with piracy, many people spread only information about the music, and not the music itself. This can be for many reasons—guilt over theft, size limitations in email accounts, or just plain laziness (which can never be underestimated). When positive comments about music are sent among friends, they often lead to legal, profitable consumption of the song, either streaming or paid ownership. Negative remarks will just as rapidly prevent sales.

Social networking sites have become more than just entertainment, and have evolved into primary communication platforms. Looking at these sites as places for people to gather and find others with likeminded interests misses its true importance. Sites like MySpace and Facebook make it easy to publicly disseminate any information a person wishes to share about himself. It can be what he did today or about the party he is throwing. An often used feature of music sharing on these pages also helps to rapidly spread individual personal preferences to large numbers of people. Most of the sites featuring music also generate royalties, including sites like Imeem, which allows the user to listen to multiple songs on demand.

On these sites, as well as other independent sites, blogs are now the norm. These create an online record of a person's experiences to the degree in which he wants to share them. Music can often be explicitly mentioned in these blogs, and most fans associate this sort of comment with viral word of mouth. However, most mentions are more casual in nature. Bloggers can offhandedly describe the music they were listening to either at the time they wrote the blog post, or at the immediate time of an event. Either way, the writer is more likely to mention the music that feels shareable, regardless of whether that was the exact music they were hearing at the moment they describe.

THE BRIDGED GENERATION GAP

The frequency of communication opportunities and multitude of communication platforms has also bridged a generation gap, and made for interesting new dynamics between children and parents. In recent years, the term "Helicopter Parents" has sprung up to describe these new relationships in which technology has allowed parents to always be close to their offspring. With so many ways to talk to each other, it is not uncommon for a child to have some form of technological communication with his parents daily, even well into his mid-twenties. This is a huge fundamental shift, as prior to this, most children welcomed the break from their parents at turning eighteen and entering college or the work force. This age group previously prided itself on infrequent parental communications, and tried hard to establish its independence. Today, the opposite is true, and many young adults are very open with their parents about all aspects of their lives.

While sociologists focus on these communications as they revolve around work, school, and health issues (sex, drugs, etc.), these conversations also include the children's entertainment choices. Since entertainment is a large topic of discussion among their peers, kids and young adults share their opinions in regular conversations with their parents. These can range from talking about the songs they personally like, to the child recommending entertainment choices to the parent as something he might enjoy.

This has now bridged a generation gap for music that used to take months, if not years, for record labels and artists to build. Parents, who are usually too busy to concern themselves with album release dates and new artists, now get relevant information about musical choices more rapidly. An artist such as James Blunt experienced his big leap into U.S. stardom after he appeared on "The Oprah Winfrey Show." Prior to that, though, he had already sold nearly a million records. Many of them were likely to this group of parents who discovered James Blunt through their children, who discovered him on countless music sites. A process that previously might have played out over several years and a couple of albums now occurred in about six months.

THE VOLUME OF MUSIC

While the methods of communication have exploded, and the number of communication points a person has in a day has increased exponentially, there is still a finite amount of communication one can have. As such, the music recommendations one can give are also finite. Each week, more then 10,000 songs are released from an array of sources at a variety of levels. There is no chance anyone could actually hear all 10,000 songs in any given week. The average song length would have to be about sixty seconds, and the listener could never sleep. Then, of the number of songs a person can actually expect to listen to, how many would the person actually like? And, of the ones he likes, how many would the person like enough to recommend to someone else?

Assume that through all that there is one song that a person likes enough to recommend. If he is a reasonably social person, he might recommend it to twenty friends. But what if those twenty friends also had one song that they liked enough to recommend? Now this group has twenty song recommendations to process. By the definitions we started with, the initial individual liked only one song from all his inputs. This means that he possibly heard, but ultimately rejected, the other nineteen songs from the group. The rest of the group could possibly have done the same. Then this process repeats every week. And that favorite song from week one has to compete with the song from week two. If it does not hold up for a second week of recommendation, the value goes away. That song then ceases to grow in popularity and revenue potential within that social network.

While this scenario is over simplified, it is actually close to the best-case scenario an artist may have for his song to be disseminated via word of mouth. Tastemakers often have a large capacity to retain an even bigger pool of song recommendations. This works as much against them as it does for them. By disseminating a wide variety of choices, they often find the recipient has a difficult choice in deciding which recommendation should be adopted into his musical canon. Tastemakers also have a habit of infusing new choices into their lexicon to keep "on top of the scene." As with the previous scenario, this usually means that today's recommendation is yesterday's forgotten favorite. It also means that it is unlikely that the tastemaker will repeatedly mention a musical recommendation enough to have resonance to a significant number of recipients. It will only stick if that same recommendation comes from multiple tastemakers at approximately the same time, presuming the person also has direct contact with multiple tastemakers.

Other tastemakers will have difficulty even coming up with one succinct choice. Ask a tastemaker to give you only one musical recommendation, and he will usually be hard-pressed to do so. Having so many options, plus a fear of making the wrong recommendation (which would diminish his tastemaker status to that individual), render it difficult for a tastemaker to even consider one choice. If he is able to make a recommendation, the choice can be easily influenced by other recent activity. He may choose something he heard in the previous hour (perhaps a song with an incomplete ending as outlined in Chapter Five), instead of something he actually preferred more, but which had been on the top of his mind the previous week.

All of these recommendation dilemmas fall under what author Barry Schwartz calls, in his book of the same name, *The Paradox of Choice*. In the book, he argues that when consumers are faced with too many choices, they actually make no choice at all. Having few options is actually more beneficial to getting a consumer engaged. This may seem antithetical to music fans and tastemakers who have the time, bandwidth, and inclination to take in large volumes of music. But that community is a small minority. That group is also unlikely to afford all the musical options it wishes to consume, and is therefore highly likely to engage in non-revenue generating musical usages. Most users do not want large volumes of musical choices. They just want a small pool that is relevant to them and will retain their interest.

Where this puts songwriters and artists is quite a predicament. The huge volume of songs being released makes reliance on word of mouth a daunting task. Yet the sharing is vital in today's musical economy for a song to generate listens, familiarity, chart positions, and royalties. The best way to overcome this obstacle is to make sure there are subtle manipulations in a song's structure and production that would induce a listener to share the song with others.

Well-timed and well-placed lyrics that whip up the listener are an easy, effective tool to spark discussion. These lyrics can appear just about anywhere in the song, but are likely most effective toward the beginning. They may need to be highlighted through the production of the song in some way. This could be through subtle techniques (raising the vocals a few dB during the designated line), or even blatant methods (dropping out the music entirely so the lyric stands out on its own). The idea is to make sure that the words have such resonance that they cause discussion, which creates rapid awareness.

"LONDON BRIDGE"

In the summer of 2006, Fergie's debut solo single, "London Bridge," achieved that multiple times within the song. It starts with a provocative exclamation ("Oh, shit!," which had to be changed for radio to "Oh, snap!") by an anonymous male chorus. At this point, only two seconds into the song, there are two discussion points for people to latch onto: The bold profanity in the original, and the inane switch to an innocuous word that would titter any kid who knew the original word. From there, Fergie's rap leads to the line, "I'm Fergie Ferg and me love you long time." That also gets attention for multiple reasons: The film reference (*Full Metal Jacket*), the prostitution allusion (from the character that spoke the line in the movie), the previous song that sampled that line (2 Live Crew's "Me So Horny"), and a potential debate about whether those words are essentially racist. The line is punctuated through production by dropping out the bass beat, and including only a mixed-down gong and chimes. By the time it gets to the disposable (and infinitely discussable) chorus line, "How come every time you come around/My London, London bridge want to go down," the song contains a plethora of discussable elements. With the very catchy, insistent hook on top of it, there is little surprise that the song was one of the biggest hits of that summer.

Much like the lyrical elements in "London Bridge," the discussion points do not have to be subtle. A cheap, but effective, ploy is to utilize provocative, even pornographic lyrics. Their shock value has diminished over time, but that does not mean that the well-timed lyric in the right environment would not provoke and gain attention. In the late 1990s, even as drug use was no longer shocking to most people, the band Buckcherry garnered a lot of attention for their debut single, "Lit Up," with a chorus that repeats the line, "I love the cocaine." On its own, the line may not have provoked, but in particular social circles, it really caused people to pay attention to the group.

Politically active lines can also stir a lot of emotion with specific audiences. Despite a lot of similarities between Vietnam and Iraq, many musicians did not write lyrics pointedly against the Iraq war to the degree the previous generation did during Vietnam. A primary reason was the fear of alienation. The wisdom held it was better to be vague and reach a wide audience than opinionated and reach a specific audience. For the purposes of word of mouth, provocation is actually a positive attribute, as it will drive people to discuss that song. The criteria in which a song can be #1 in either popularity or revenue have steadily come down. Now there is a chance for a non-mass appeal song to reach mass-appeal numbers if exposed correctly. Provoking in a particular way can prove very beneficial in getting that song noticed.

One of the few artists who did position his stance on the U.S. war on terror in the early stages was country star Toby Keith. He reached a much bigger cultural awareness with his 2002 hit, "Courtesy of the Red, White, & Blue." The song starts with direct, sentimental lyrics about past military glory both personal and broad. It then kicks into high gear with snappy, quotable lyrics about the Statue of Liberty shaking her fist, and rhyming hell with Mother Freedom's bell. This all builds to the line, "'Cuz we'll put a boot in your ass/It's the American way," which drew attention and controversy. Each of those lyrical bon mots was infinitely discussable, and took Toby to a much greater height of popularity.

INSTRUMENTAL RIFFS

If it makes sense for a particular artist or song, the talking point can also be an instrumental solo. As songs have gotten more perfunctory, sample-reliant and computerized, the placement of extremely memorable instrumental passages has largely vanished from popular music. Very few songs in the late 1990s through today had significant memorable guitar licks like those found in "Layla," "Let's Go Crazy," or "Smells Like Teen Spirit." Guitar solos are not the only type that can be memorable, as talented musicians can likely come up with unforgettable keyboard solos, horn riffs, or even the formerly clichéd live drum solo. The right song with the right instrumental hook will likely have a large leg up in enabling that song to be disseminated through word of mouth.

That instrumental riff can also be something completely foreign. It's been nearly twenty years since the band Jackyl took a chainsaw and made it an instrument in their one hit, "The Lumberjack." Unique twists such as that change what is defined as an instrument, and can surely get people talking about the unexpected nature of those sounds. The ability to manipulate these new, unusual sounds via computer programming brings a much higher likelihood that any sound can work musically within a particular song. In recent years, this technique has only been actively pursued within beat programming. But its implementation should be just as frequent in organic song production to make the title more distinct.

Placement of the solo can likewise spur people into lengthy discussions, if it comes at a point that forces people to pay attention to it. Depending on the song, this could be the intro, the outro, or a more traditional "after the second chorus" placement. Much like other aspects discussed here, the solo can also have maximum impact by being placed in an unexpected spot. The surprise timing of a well written, extremely well played instrumental solo can be strong enough to command attention and discussion.

In recent years, these elements have largely been absent from popular music, mostly because they went against the programming philosophies of nearly all radio stations. Radio had a directive to make sure the musical sound was flat and consistent. This was done with the intention of hoping that the listener would not switch the station to a competitor.

Radio, then, would not play songs with attention-grabbing solos, or if they were played, those solos were often edited out, thereby neutering their ability to have a commanding reach as a cultural discussion point.

The new distribution techniques for music actually favor the opposite direction. The blandness now required by radio becomes a song's greatest liability. If the song maintains a consistent sound with very few distinguishing characteristics from other songs in its genre, it will have a very low likelihood of being discussed in any capacity. Little discussion will make it much harder for that song to gain relevant traction for repeat listenership, thereby minimizing familiarity and revenue opportunities. The only exceptions are songs of the mellow, background variety outlined in Chapter Eleven. By their definition, this style is not created to encourage sharing, and therefore the listeners of this style are unlikely to do so.

BLOCKING OTHER SONGS FROM THE DISCUSSION

Once the proper elements are in place, the hope is that song will then be shared and discussed. The crucial reason to maximize a song for sharing is that it makes it less likely for yet another song to be shared. Today's music consumer has nearly infinite choices, but limited bandwidth. Establishing a foothold for discussion of a particular song is as much about boxing out the competition as it is about making sure a particular song is good enough to be heard countless times.

Major record companies practiced a variation of this for years by establishing an intricate payola system with radio. With nationwide radio penetration costing hundreds of thousands of dollars for viable, prolonged airplay, it virtually assured that those without cash (i.e. the little guy) could not penetrate and create popular music. The difference in today's musical environment is that dollars will only get an artist and song so far in awareness and penetration. To truly box out competition, one must manage other songs out of the discussion. The more interesting a song, and the more quality it has to lead into dialogue and sharing, the more the competition does not come into play. With that, the song in focus can reap more revenues and chart positioning.

Giving the song a distinct voice will certainly help in generating those discussion points and getting the leg up. However, the song itself cannot be made up solely of these engaging points, as that would likely make it so impenetrable that most people would fail to embrace it. Rather, these points should be used as spices throughout to add the zest and kick that enhance a listener's interest. Most important, though, there is still the need for broad appeal. While "Long Tail" enthusiasts talk about the ability to generate revenues for years to come, the hit song needs a lot more. To truly be a hit for the ages, the song has to be adaptable enough to encompass so many different listeners and listening experiences, that even the word "broad" might not cover it.

15

UNIVERSAL SONGS

FOR MULTIPLE USES

The subtle changes in song structures that have been mentioned in previous chapters are all extremely effective tools that will enhance a song's popularity and ability to generate revenue. Not every song will be able to embrace every single technique, but adopting several of them will likely yield significant results over other songs that fail to employ those techniques. However, those ideas on their own may not be enough to make it successful. To achieve that, the song must be malleable enough to be utilized in multiple places.

For example, think about most romantic comedy movies. In many ways, they are among the most predictable movies that Hollywood makes. A lot of them do not even bring in spectacular box office numbers. Yet they consistently get made, for Hollywood finds these movies a much safer bet for uses and forms outside the theatre. After the theatrical run maximizes that audience (usually couples on dates), the movie has little difficulty appearing on airplanes, where the banality makes it more acceptable to a larger group. A similar process occurs when a couple makes a rental or pay-per-view choice. Rather than each going for a unique choice that only one individual wants, they instead opt for a clichéd romantic comedy that is mildly acceptable to both people. By the time the movie makes it to free TV, there is a larger chance that the person has seen that movie over others. Since the viewer has a higher likelihood of being sucked into watching the movie again, these movies will air more often on television. Think about how many of these movies appear on TV over the weekend.

The potential success of making music mellower to fit into that background was already covered in Chapter Eleven. The example that artists can take away from Hollywood is to make music that is widely adaptable for multiple usages. It works equally well in theatres, on airplanes, for video rentals, and on TV, in both pay and free forms. It also works as a suitable selection for people when they are bored, or when multiple people need to have an agreeable choice. The science most Hollywood studios put into making sure these films have multiple uses is deep, and figures into the film's adaptability in countries outside the United States.

IDENTIFYING SITUATIONS

Intentionally coming up with songs that can be used in multiple places is relatively easy. The first step is to cover situations in which the average person listens to music. The walking beat, previously covered in Chapter Thirteen, is an example of how tempo can affect the audience of a song. But what are people doing while they are walking? A lot of people are going to onerous destinations, such as work or school. They are also going away from those destinations at other times. Either situation would likely result in different types of songs that the listener would want to hear. People also listen on airplanes to combat boredom. In that situation, they are more apt to spend time skipping between songs, since they have fewer distractions. This is not a time for a user to hear dull songs.

Nor is it an effective time for a song about a plane crash. This advice may seem intuitive and obvious (and not a common issue in songwriting), but a song about plane crashes would almost certainly have minimal plays on an airplane. This is a main reason why plane crashes rarely figure in movies and, if so, they are edited out before airings on a plane. Similarly, the person going to and from work probably does not want to be reminded of the drudgery of his job. A song that might remind him of why he is doing the work in the first place (looking forward to the weekend, how much he loves his spouse or family, escapist ideals, etc.), or songs that sympathize with the working man's plight, would probably result in more play events than a whining song about how bad modern life is.

When you add up all those situations, inspirational songs are more likely to experience plays than negative ones. That is not to say that negative songs (falling out of love, life is dreary, etc.) will not find a significant audience. But these songs do have a lower likelihood of experiencing a play event that generates royalties. In the past, these songs had only a slight disadvantage to positive songs, as they could make the same amount of money simply by selling enough, regardless of how many times that purchase was heard. Now that songs must have multiple listens to chart, become familiar, and earn revenue, those songs will likely be much less profitable than before.

At home uses also become vital to increasing plays. While this conjures an image of kids listening to online music while doing homework or surfing the web, a much larger usage will likely be in children's music. Any parent can tell you that a children's CD is usually the most listened to disc in the house. These CDs generally experience good sales, but if tracked on a per-listen basis, they would have given the consumer more value for his money than a pop CD. Placed into the digital world of music consumption, where each of these plays is tracked for royalties, the dollars earned will probably grow at a higher exponential rate than other genres.

Other uses at home include housework, romantic encounters (both tame and explicit), and dinner parties. A lot of usage also now takes place either during web surfing or general household computer usage. Common activities in these situations include reading/sending emails, checking social networking sites, finding information, banking, playing games, doing homework, and watching pornography. This does not mean songs should be written about these subjects explicitly. Much like the person going to work, listeners are most comfortable with music that fits the situation, but is not *about* that situation. With a listener playing an online game, there are only a few (such as Solitaire) that are generally played in a calm fashion. Many games have a clock/timer that puts pressure on the player to achieve a goal quickly. Songs that help increase a person's anxiety level may produce positive results in the listener's ability to channel good stress and be successful at the game. He may not necessarily notice that the right song helped him win the game, but he very well may feel "off" when the wrong song plays.

Since these are generally played on the computer, there will be increased situations where people will be listening to music off of streams, instead of playing songs downloaded on the hard drive. This will mean that songs will have to be easily found and accessible to people on online outlets. Once again, the techniques needed to gain a leg up on online radio are going to be crucial to insure that songs garner additional plays to generate revenue.

PLAYLISTS

Many of these song plays will start occurring in greater frequency from playlists. Whether web-based or created on an individual's computer, getting a song onto multiple playlists of multiple people is crucial to insure familiarity and achieve royalties. To do that, an examination of what playlists people create is in order. A study of playlists on iTunes finds that most playlists can be grouped into the following themes: Artist specific, genre specific, soundtracks (movie, TV, and games), nostalgia, relaxation, dancing, sad emotions, event related, romantic, and inspirational.

The playlists that people are creating and playing are largely tilting toward hits or mostly positive themes. Time and external factors determine if a specific song actually becomes a hit. The themes, however, are easily manipulated today. Finding songs that play into the themes that people like to create gives extra visibility and airplay to those songs. More importantly, not creating songs within these themes will mean the songs are *not* being included on playlists, thereby cutting out a vital method in which a song can be heard and distributed.

SOUNDTRACK PLACEMENTS

The abundance of music being created by individuals has also resulted in a boom for Hollywood. Several factors have converged to create a welcome climate for artists and their songs. The explosion of digital cable channels and outlets has created an increased demand for new, original programming. With hundreds of channels needing programs that fill a week for nearly every conceivable niche, more TV shows are being created than ever before. This means that more programs need music, creating a wealth of opportunities.

The downside is that these opportunities are not often lucrative for the composer or performer. The shows themselves have very low budgets, and the fact that they draw niche audiences generally means there is not a large advertiser base from which to pull generous amounts of money. Therefore, everyone involved in the project usually accepts lower rates. Reality based programming has increased exponentially for this reason, as the viewer accepts lower quality production, which allows for dramatic cost cutting. Additionally, participants enjoy being part of the action, and are willing to accept much lower compensation than union actors.

For musicians, the lower budgets are both a blessing and a curse. Having small music budgets makes it nearly impossible for shows to commission original works. The cheaper alternative is to turn to songs that have already been created. At that point, the songs' creators can either accept or turn down the smaller figures. But there is no risk to the program creator, as he knows exactly the song he will get and whether it fits his needs.

This situation is not dramatically different from the one musicians find with online royalties. Large payments for one use will be an increasingly rare occurrence in nearly all aspects of music, and licensing is no different. Just as substantial online royalties are made by mass, repetitive usage, so are licensing royalties. Songs will be licensed multiple times across multiple shows to maximize both their exposure and revenue opportunities. The fact that networks need to fill twenty-four hours every day necessitates high levels of reruns, which can generate repeated public performance payments for the songwriter over long periods of time. The more usages obtained, the more they will be revenue generators for many years.

Much like playlists, musicians need to cater to the needs of their audience in order to secure exposure and royalties. In this case, the audience is made up of music supervisors. Musicians who think about the audience's needs and write songs for those situations will increase the likelihood that a song receives those opportunities. Music supervisors report that the needs for these programs tend to be remarkably consistent. Not surprising, they mirror the universal themes that people create playlists around: Nostalgia, dancing, sad emotions, romantic, and inspirational. One simply needs to watch any amount of TV and pay attention to the song selections to realize what types of music are being used. Supervisors also look for songs that have strong soft-to-loud dynamics (see Chapter Four) to build up dramatic tension and/or provide emotional impact in promotional spots.

With increased pressure, music supervisors need to listen to multiple songs very quickly. Therefore, adapting to their thematic needs is not enough. Making sure those songs conform to the other techniques found in this book helps them sync with the supervisor's listening habits. If the song sticks out among all the other submissions, then the song has a higher likelihood of being selected for the usage. Engaging the supervisor quickly is a high priority to securing placements.

Currently, song placement on most user-generated Internet video is not being effectively monitored or enforced. Sites like YouTube have spawned millions of amateur filmmakers who are completely unaware that utilizing music other than their own requires licensing and royalty payments. This issue will likely be resolved over time, starting with YouTube's deals with major music publishers to account for these royalties. However, the situation will remain difficult to enforce for awhile, as the sheer volume of content makes it difficult to track accounting and payment for all uses. Recent song identification software has greatly improved this process, specifically on YouTube.

As more original programming appears on the Internet from legitimate sources, a lot more opportunities for musical synchronizations will be created. As this grows, the types of programs being created will have to be carefully examined to understand the needs of these content creators. They will likely be variations of what already exists in other media, but new styles could create unique opportunities for different types of songs.

VIDEO GAME PLACEMENTS

In recent years, video game synchronization has become an important part of many artists' marketing plans. While it is ostensibly easy for a player to turn down the game's sound and play his own music, the majority of people do not, and are very comfortable playing the game as is. This inevitably results in high repetition of the songs included in the video game being played.

Video game companies are notorious for paying very little for song usage, but what the musician gets in return is repetition and familiarity. Since one cannot simply lift the song from his Xbox to his iPod without great difficulty, the repetition can easily lead to other revenue opportunities, covering the gap in lower initial revenues. These songs will also inevitably show up as favorites in the user's online streaming experiences and playlists. This will lead to those songs not only generating more streaming revenues, but also solid research for the streaming companies. This helps establish those songs as hits on those sites.

New generations of video games are utilizing devices and software with far more storage capacity than previously attained. To the consumer, this has resulted in hi-definition graphics and surround sound effects previously unachieved. For the musician, this also means increased space to include songs. In 2008, the biggest video game release, *Grand Theft Auto IV*, contained over 200 songs pre-loaded into the game. In games, music will always be important, but also secondary to the graphics and code for the game itself. Therefore, in older generation games, if the title had room for only ten songs, then that was all that was included, even if the original concept called for twenty. With increased capabilities on new devices, space for music will be less of a concern. This means that the number of songs in games will grow to numbers beyond *Grand Theft Auto IV*. With a larger song volume to draw from, initial repetition of song plays will take longer for all titles. Over time, however, the increased musical variety will eliminate boredom from the music, and keep players more engaged in the game's music.

Much like film and TV supervisors, the songs selected will be the ones that fit the situations. In most cases, the needs are fast, aggressive songs, along with mid-tempo hip-hop songs. The soft pop sound that might work well for TV usages has little application in this media. The uses are very specific to drive the player's game forward.

For the artists and songs that fit this mold, the competition is also great. The exposure—combined with the prestige many artists receive from their peers for appearing in key titles—leads to significant pressure for songs to be included. As in TV and film, this results in a high volume of submissions that often have to be picked through and tested against the game in a very short period of time. This means that these aggressive songs have to stick out and be instantly synchronous with the game. If the song takes a long time to engage the user or to license from multiple copyright holders, there is a high likelihood it will not make the final consideration pile.

ADVERTISING PLACEMENTS

Despite an increase in demand for actual songs, one area that has not experienced quite the same competition is advertising. With so many channels now proliferating throughout TV, just about any product or service can make a spot that reaches its target audience. Virtually every spot contains music of some sort. This means a marked increase in both original and pre-recorded music for these commercials.

The volume increase comes from companies that previously could not afford to advertise in the network and top-tier cable game, where spots cost hundreds of thousands of dollars. If they cannot afford the expensive costs to place the spots in A-list programming, then they also do not have significant money for top-shelf music. The advantage is that, with the right spot and target market, a new song can establish familiarity and garner fees, though minimal.

The chances a song would springboard into as much familiarity or as many ancillary streams as in video games and top TV placement is much smaller. The usage is usually limited to thirty seconds. Also, the repetition is at the whim of the advertiser, not the end user to whom the repetition is aimed. An advantage, though, is that there is a larger volume of usage in unforeseen programming that can result in much larger public performance fees than usual.

Competition on the whole is much smaller in advertising placements. Some of this still stems from artists' perception of "selling out" in advertising, though this pool has noticeably shrunk in recent years. Another reason comes from music usually being an afterthought in the spot's production. Unless the ad is focused on a particular hit song or artist, music is not in the forefront of the creative process. As such, there is not as much heavy consideration for music as one finds in other areas of film and TV. Often, an internal person at an ad agency selects a favorite song, finds it is affordable, and applies it. Ad agencies and spot producers rarely solicit actively for submissions like film and TV music supervisors.

There is also less competition because existing music generally does not fit most advertising. Like other placements, the tracks selected must fit the usage requirements, and for advertising, this usually means mid-tempo, happy songs with just enough energy to keep the user interested. Almost always, songs that are loud, depressing, slow, or too fast are not considered. Chances are if the song generates a negative emotional response from the listener, the advertiser will not desire it.

In recent years, much has been made of "hip" independent bands receiving more placements in advertising spots. While this has largely been the case, it has also coincided with the same music becoming softer and more melodic. The more challenging songs in the underground are still not being licensed. It cannot be emphasized enough that playing to the needed uses will yield the strongest results for licensing opportunities.

For all cases of music synchronization, a specific sound is desired for usage. The usage will rarely be tailored to fit the song—the song must be tailored to fit the usage. To accommodate the most possible uses, the songs must have as many of the elements detailed above. The more songs deviate from these universal themes, the more the songs will not be placed. For most music creators, this is nearly sacrilegious. The last thing an artist wants to do is to actively consider commercial applications for his music in the creation process. Yet this is a fine way to create, and one should never begrudge an artist who actively pursues his craft in this regard.

The main difference today concerns the financial streams from which the artist derives his income. In previous years, large forms of revenue came from sales of the recorded work. As these income streams shrink, one needs to look to the growth areas to make up the shortfall. Digital and mobile income is looking to close the gap considerably, but projections are showing that these streams will not cover the shortfall in most situations.

The biggest area of growth is licensing. These opportunities are increasing rapidly and look to grow further over time. Keeping these opportunities in mind during the creation process will be akin to thinking about a song's "radio potential" in the past. It will likely not be the primary focus, but it should be a significant consideration point. This will affect everything from structure to arrangements to lyrical choices. Without it, the song creators will be putting significant portions of their income potential at risk.

Songs that speak to a universal nature always had a leg up in the marketplace. Competition for those spots, however, was never as active as it is in today's digital world. Niche songs will continue to find a modest foothold, as there are "Long Tail" uses that can yield some success. In looking at a niche song's revenue potential, however, artists are taking a big gamble. To guarantee a song's financial success, and to increase its potential to be heard repetitively and remembered for years to come, the creator should aim for a broad appeal. It is an artist's best bet.

CODA

A word to the wise: Do not try everything in this book. Admittedly, the steps taken in this book are plentiful, and I would venture to guess that consciously applying all of these techniques into one outburst of music might not yield the best results. Instead, think of these thoughts as a jumping off point. Read and re-read the book until the ideas become second nature. Then, just naturally adapt the techniques as they fit any individual song.

More importantly than the *what*, think about the *why*. With the way technology is moving, portions of this book may already be outdated by the time you read this. Certainly, new techniques will arise that will become popular overnight. New methodologies will arise, and entire new pieces of hardware will be invented.

But listen closely to what is written underneath every word in this book: Pay attention to your audience. Certain music becomes popular at certain periods not specifically because of how great the music is, but also because of various other sociological factors. For example, could there be another Grateful Dead or Phish with a traveling caravan of fans driving to every show when gas costs four dollars a gallon? Can a poor, destitute band that needs to squat for shelter before it gets discovered actually make it if its members can't pay for Internet access?

Most importantly, how can anyone rise above the noise and clutter? In my travels, the worst thing that I find with most music I hear is that it is neither good nor bad. It is just there. It fails to engage or make a statement of any kind. If I were in a bar listening to the artist play, I probably would not leave. But nor would I pay enough attention to remember the person playing. This may be harsh, but it is also the truth. And this is coming from someone who gets paid to enjoy music.

This has to be stressed because some people will undoubtedly challenge the analytical approach to hit making that this book adopts. These people would love to cling to the notion that their music deserves to be a hit without tainting or strategy—just straight from the soul. This is a perfectly sound strategy if you happen to be as gifted as John Lennon or Jimi Hendrix, among others. The sad truth is that musicians who are truly that gifted are an extreme rarity. For most musicians who want to work and make it their profession, being anywhere below genius level requires some compromise.

Even Andy Warhol had to compromise. If you dig into his early biography, you will find that Andy essentially created a style of work, showed that work, and then when the industry critiqued it, he shifted his style just enough to placate said industry while still keeping it his own. Along the way, he made other works that were totally his own, but he always knew to have a commercial side that brought in funds to truly practice his craft.

But whether or not you adapt one, all, or none of these thoughts, please make sure you understand the underlying message. To succeed, you must find a way into your audience's life. They are not looking for you. You need to make them want to come to you. To do that, think about how they consume music as a whole in every way, and craft music for it. Think specifically about the technology and how that engages the listener, or perhaps disengages them.

Above all, do not be shy. The introverted genius in the bedroom always had a hard time being discovered. Just because YouTube can bring a bedroom to the world does not mean the world will tune into his bedroom. If that genius does not make a genuine effort to write songs that attract an audience on first listen—or actively place the song in places and avenues where it can be discovered—it will remain undiscovered.

More than anything, this book should inspire. It should inspire someone to create more music so he can try more things. Inspire someone to get off his chair and actively show people his music. Inspire someone to think more about how to make his music more attractive to others. Inspire everyone to take stock of where music listening actually is today and not live with blinders on, dreaming of the good old days where music was given a chance.

Guess what…every song is given a chance. But with the volume of music available, that chance of success grew from the odds of the Pick 3 lottery to the odds of the Powerball. Consider that everyone will adapt the ideas in this book differently. That is a good thing. Others will never adapt to the ideas because they either disagree or they do not read the book. That is fine as well. And some of them may have more success without adopting any of these rules.

The path of music creation is not a straight, nor firmly paved one. If it were, every friend and relative would not look at you strangely when you mention that it is your life's goal. My hope is that what you have read inspires you to make those subtle changes that improve your music just enough to make music more successful for us all.

ACKNOWLEDGMENTS

Many people have touched and influenced this book in so many ways. It has come from many significant discussions I have had over the years with many people in all facets of the music business. These extremely spirited debates not only allowed me the chance to shape the ideas in *Futurehit.DNA*, but also showed me that there are a lot of smart, creative people in the music business who have been trying to turn things around for many years.

Chief among those is Spencer Proffer, my brother, mentor and spiritual advisor. Your encouragement and aid in getting this book to the industry-at-large has been invaluable. Your ability to connect any project on multiple levels is what gave me the additional drive to make this a game-changing book.

I have always known that Daniel Glass is one of the good guys in the business, and his help on this book has proven that beyond words. From our first discussions at a restaurant in Paris as I wrote the first draft, to poring over the final edit, his advice and guidance has been invaluable.

Many others perused various drafts of the book and offered a ton of insightful comments: Paul Freundlich, Billy Mann, and Richard Palmese chief among them.

The writings and friendship of Moses Avalon has also certainly influenced this book. The success of his books gave me the confidence to know that my own could succeed, and our thorough debates allowed many theories to be as bulletproof as possible over the years.

Everyone I have ever worked for has always given me encouragement, knowledge and resources to excel in this business. Their support has been key to my success: Peter Cohen, Dave Goldberg, John Mazzacco, John Peterson, Marcus Peterzell, Brian Philips, Robert Roback, Ian Rogers, Bob Skoro, Van Toffler, Chris Wheatley, John Wyatt.

The people who have worked for me have also played a role in shaping this book. Their hard work, dedication, and diversity of thought, mind, and spirit has enabled us to consistently change the way people get their music and truly move many artists forward.

My team behind the scenes has been key to making sure nothing gets forgotten. This includes my exceptional book editor Alanna Nash, whose advice helped me get this book across the finish line. Matt Greenberg, of Greenberg Traurig, has been more than just an attorney, but also a great friend. Making sure the business is taken care of is the key team of Kelley Rivera and Karen Block at Karen Block & Co., Bill Grantham, of Greenberg Traurig, and Mishawn Nolan and Heidi Feldman at Stone/Rosenblatt/Cha. I am honored and humbled by Hugh Syme's contribution to the cover design. Katy Maki was also instrumental in getting this book across the finish line. And the finish line itself courtesy of the Topspin team: Ian, Shamal Ranasinghe, Kami Knake, and James Lamberti. Then there's the general advice of the best unofficial legal team I ever had: Brooke Chaffin, Mark Walker, and Jim Pitaro.

Finally, I don't think a thank you to my family would do justice to what I owe them. My parents always encouraged me to follow the music business as a career, even when it did not look like the greatest idea in the world. My wife, Linda, did not just support the writing of this book, but allowed me many trips and isolated weekends so I could have the focus to get everything done. Your support and love mean more than I can ever say. Last, I thank our daughter Alexandria, whose love for life and music will likely shape the Future Hits.

SOURCES AND

FURTHER

INFORMATION

BOOKS

Anderson, Chris. *The Long Tail: Why The Future Of Business Is Selling Less of More*. Hyperion. 2006.

Fitch, Catherine A., and Ruggles, Steven. *The Ties That Bind: Perspectives On Marriage and Cohabitation*: 64

Gladwell, Malcolm. *Blink: The Power of Thinking Without Thinking*. Little, Brown and Company. 2005.

Lanza, Joseph. *Elevator Music*. Picador. 1994.

Schwartz, Barry. *The Paradox Of Choice: Why More Is Less*. HarperCollins. 2004.

Surowiecki, James. *The Wisdom Of Crowds*. Doubleday. 2004.

Whitburn, Joel. *Top Pop Singles 1955-2002*. Record Research. 2003.

ARTICLES

"About The Foundation." Rhythm & Blues Foundation.
<http://www.rhythm-n-blues.org/pubs/101_531_1401.CFM>.

Broughton, Frank. "Francis Grasso." DJ History. 4 February 1999. < http://www.djhistory.com/interviews/francis-grasso>

Broughton, Frank. "Jimmy Savile." DJ History. 20 May 2004. < http://www.djhistory.com/interviews/jimmy-savile>

Christman, Ed. "Retail Track: If Map Policies End, Loss-leadering May Return." Billboard. 13 May 2000.
<http://www.allbusiness.com/retail-trade/miscellaneous-retail-retail-stores-not/4636178-1.html>.

Cross, David. "A History Of The Development Of DJ Mixer Features; An S&TS Perspective." December 2003.
<http://www.zenknee.com/DJ_Mixer_History.pdf>.

Dunham, Will. "Disco Tune 'Stayin' Alive' Could Save Your Life." Reuters. 16 October 2008.
<http://news.yahoo.com/s/nm/20081016/od_nm/us_heart_be_egees>

"History of Vinyl." <
http://www.vinylrecordscollector.co.uk/text/index.html>.

"In Re: Compact Disc Minimum Advertised Price Antitrust Litigation." MDL Docket No. 1361.
<news.findlaw.com/hdocs/docs/recordcos/cdmap61303stlmnt.pdf>.

"The Infinite Dial 2008: Radio's Digital Platforms." Arbitron/Edison Media Research. 2008.

<http://www.arbitron.com/downloads/digital_radio_study_2
008.pdf>

Kieskowski, Ellie. "AFTRA Rules Cause Radio Stations to
Pull Streams." Streaming Media.
<http://www.streamingmedia.com/article.asp?id=7105>.

Kraemer, David J.M., Macrae, C. Neil, Green, Adam E., and
Kelley, William M. "Musical imagery: Sound of silence
activates auditory cortex." Nature. 10 March 2005.
<http://www.nature.com/nature/journal/v434/n7030/full/434
158a.html>.

Oxenford, David. "Copyright Royalty Board Releases
Decision – Rates are Going Up Significantly." Broadcast
Law Blog.
<http://www.broadcastlawblog.com/archives/internet-radio-
copyright-royalty-board-releases-decision-rates-are-going-
up-significantly.html>.

Oxenford, David. "Satellite Radio Music Royalty
Reconsideration Denied By Copyright Royalty Board –
What a Difference A Standard Makes." Broadcast Law Blog.
<http://www.broadcastlawblog.com/archives/internet-radio-
satellite-radio-music-royalty-reconsideration-denied-by-
copyright-royalty-board-what-a-difference-a-standard-
makes.html>.

Quail, Mark. "Music, Money and Songwriters: ASCAP and
its Relation to Jazz and R&B Songwriters in the 1930s."
Antique Phonograph News.
<http://www.capsnews.org/apn2007-3.htm>.

"Record Companies Settle FTC Charges of Restraining
Competition in CD Music Market." Federal Trade
Commission.
<http://www.ftc.gov/opa/2000/05/cdpres.shtm>.

Sivers, Derek. "Cover Songs In Digital Distribution."
CDBaby.
<http://cdbaby.org/stories/05/05/14/1931484.html>.

"Spot Load Study 2005: Managing Radio Commercial
Inventories For Advertisers and Listeners." Edison Media
Research.
<http://www.arbitron.com/downloads/spotloadppt2005.pdf>.

"Summary of the Determination of the Librarian of Congress
on Rates and Terms for Webcasting and Ephemeral
Recordings." Library Of Congress.
<http://www.copyright.gov/carp/webcasting_rates_final.html
>.

Taintor, Callie. "Chronology: Technology and the Music
Industry." *Frontline.* <
http://www.pbs.org/wgbh/pages/frontline/shows/music/insid
e/cron.html>.

Totilo, Stephen. "'Grand Theft Auto IV' Music Man
Explains How Those 214 Songs Made The Soundtrack."
<http://www.mtvasia.com/News/200805/05015842.html>.

"Vinyl." *BBC.* <
http://www.bbc.co.uk/music/features/vinyl/>.

"Visualizing MUSICAL STRUCTURE for existing Pianola
presentations." The PIANOLA News.
<http://www.wiscasset.net/artcraft/oldnews7.htm>.

Webster, Tom. "Online Radio Reaches 33 Million
Americans Per Week." Edison Media Research.
<http://www.edisonresearch.com/home/archives/2008/03/onl
ine_radio_re.php>.

"Youtube.com Accounted for 1 out of Every 3 U.S. Online Videos Viewed In January." PR Newswire. <http://www.syscon.com/read/519613.htm>.

WEBSITES

www.allmusic.com
www.bigchampagne.com
www.djhistory.com
www.gracenote.com
www.rhapsody.com
www.soundexchange.com
www.topspinmedia.com
www.wikipedia.org

ABOUT THE AUTHOR

Jay Frank is currently the SVP of Music Strategy for CMT, a division of MTV Networks. At CMT, he oversees the implementation of music across all platforms, including TV, web, mobile and VOD. The new synergy he is developing is changing the face of country music as he identifies future country hits through active monitoring of all platforms.

Jay Frank has also managed music programming, along with artist and label relations for Yahoo! Music, formerly known as LAUNCH. His ability to find hits early also led to Yahoo! Music becoming instrumental in breaking many acts in their early stages. This ability has also led Yahoo! Music to be a leading indicator of the future success for an artist.

Jay is a constant fixture at music industry conferences, often called upon as an expert on Digital Music programming. He has been featured on panels throughout the world such as South by Southwest, MIDEM, Billboard Radio Monitor, DemExpo, MusExpo, Music & Media (Finland), Jupiter Plug.In, Canadian Music Week, R&R, Winter Music Conference, CMJ and several others. He is also regularly called to lend his expertise to press stories with most major media outlets, including CNN, Entertainment Weekly, USA Today, Rolling Stone, The Washington Post, Billboard, Wired, and many more.

Jay has also been senior music director at The Box Music Network, marketing and A&R for Ignition Records, managed a live music venue, programmed broadcast radio stations and created two local music video shows.

Futurehit.dna is his first book.

20.00

CPSIA information can be obtained at www.ICGtesting.com
Printed in the USA
LVOW121633131212

311547LV00003B/438/P

9 780615 285702